FAMOUS PEOPLE
QUIZ BOOK

By the same author

The All-British Quiz Book
Progressive Brain-Teasing Quizzes
Test Your Word Power

Uniform with this book

FAMOUS PEOPLE QUIZ BOOK

Compiled by
John G. Barton

PAPERFRONTS

ELLIOT RIGHT WAY BOOKS
KINGSWOOD SURREY U.K.

Made and Printed in Great Britain by
Cox & Wyman Ltd, London, Reading and Fakenham

To
Anne – Louise

IN THE SAME SERIES

If you love quizzes, you will love:

ENIGMA 1000 QUIZ BOOK
THE ALL BRITISH QUIZ BOOK
PROGRESSIVE BRAIN-TEASING QUIZZES
WORD QUIZ BOOK

If you enjoy puzzles, word, number, logic, etc., you will enjoy:

PUZZLES AND TEASERS FOR THE EASY-CHAIR
PUZZLES AND TEASERS FOR EVERYONE
TEST YOUR WORD POWER

If you relish crosswords, you will relish:

CROSSWORDS FOR THE DEVOTEE
CROSSWORDS FOR THE ENTHUSIAST

Contents

Introduction

Most of the famous people of the past, and many of the present day, appear in this book. There are questions on where they were born, what they achieved, where they lived, what they said, where they went and where they were buried.

I have tried to pose questions which the reader will find interesting and stimulating, not too hard and not too easy. Questions that are too easy and can be answered by everybody are as useless as questions that are too hard and can be answered by nobody.

To all those who have expressed appreciation of my previous quiz books I offer this new one in the hope that it will give further enjoyment.

I should like to thank my wife for reading the manuscript, the publishers for their encouragement, and the Encyclopaedia Britannica for permission to use their latest edition as a final authority for facts and figures.

Though every care has been taken errors may occur in this type of book. If any reader finds an error and is kind enough to write to the publisher the author will be grateful.

John G. Barton

Architects and Engineers

1. Name: (a) the English architect, born in Sweden, who designed Somerset House in London; (b) the Scottish architect who designed Syon House and Osterley Park.

2. Which of these artists were also architects: Bernini, Michelangelo, Reynolds, Goya, Titian, Raphael?

3. Name: (a) the dramatist who designed Blenheim Palace; (b) the astronomer who designed St. Paul's Cathedral.

4. What have the following in common: Lancelot Brown, Humphry Repton, William Kent?

5. What nationality were these famous architects: (a) Le Corbusier; (b) Gaudi; (c) Gropius; (d) Frank Lloyd Wright?

6. Who designed these: (a) Houses of Parliament; (b) Coventry Cathedral; (c) Regent's Park?

7. Name: (a) the theatrical designer who designed the Banqueting House, Whitehall; (b) the town planner who re-designed the Royal Pavilion, Brighton.

8. Name the great canal engineer who was illiterate.

9. Who was the engineer and designer of the Suez Canal?

10. Who designed the two bridges across the Menai Straits?

11. Who designed these bridges: (a) Clifton Suspension; (b) Forth railway; (c) Pont Cysyllte; (d) Royal Border?

12. Name the great eighteenth-century road-builder who was blind.

Architects and Engineers

1. (*a*) Sir William Chambers; (*b*) Robert Adam.

2. Bernini, Michelangelo and Raphael.

3. (*a*) Sir John Vanbrugh;   (*b*) Sir Christopher Wren.

4. They were all famous landscape designers.

5. (*a*) French; (*b*) Spanish; (*c*) German, later American; (*d*) American.

6. (*a*) Sir Charles Barry and   (*b*) Sir Basil Spence;
   A. W. Pugin;   (*c*) John Nash.

7. (*a*) Inigo Jones;   (*b*) John Nash.

8. James Brindley.

9. Ferdinand de Lesseps.

10. The suspension bridge for road traffic was designed by Thomas Telford, and the Britannia railway bridge by Robert Stephenson.

11. (*a*) I. K. Brunel;   (*b*) Sir Benjamin Baker;
    (*c*) Thomas Telford;   (*d*) Robert Stephenson.

12. John Metcalfe ('Blind Jack of Knaresborough').

Aviators and Aeronauts

1. Who first crossed the English Channel by air?

2. What historic event occurred on November 21st, 1783, at Paris?

3. Name the two great pioneers of aeronautics of the nineteenth century.

4. What historic aeroplane flights were achieved by: (a) the Wright brothers in 1903; (b) Louis Blériot in 1909?

5. Who was Count von Zeppelin?

6. (a) Who made the first direct non-stop crossing of the Atlantic? (b) Who made the first solo non-stop crossing?

7. Who was Baron Manfred von Richthofen?

8. What was the achievement of the American Wiley Post in 1933?

9. Who was the famous woman aviator who flew from England to Australia in 1930?

10. Here are some famous flying 'aces' of the two World Wars. Give their nationalities and state in which of the two wars they became famous: Rickenbacker, Gibson, Bishop, Bader, Immelmann, Ball, Malan, Cheshire.

11. What historic flights were made by: (a) Richard Byrd in 1926 and 1929; (b) Ross Smith in 1919; (c) Colonel Cody in 1908 (16th October)?

12. Whose aircraft was named *Spirit of St. Louis*?

Answers

Aviators and Aeronauts

1. Blanchard and Jeffries in a balloon in 1785.

2. The world's first human aerial voyage, in a Montgolfier hot-air balloon, by de Rozier and Marquis d'Arlandes.

3. Sir George Cayley (1773–1857) who constructed the first man-carrying glider, and Otto Lilienthal (1848–1896) who was the first to fly successfully in gliders.

4. (a) the first controlled, powered flight; (b) the first cross-Channel flight.

5. von Zeppelin (1838–1917) was the pioneer constructor of the airships named after him.

6. (a) John Alcock and Arthur Whitten-Brown in a Vickers Vimy in June, 1919; (b) Colonel Charles Lindbergh from New York to Paris in 1927.

7. A German fighter-plane 'ace' of the first World War.

8. He was the first man to fly solo round the world. The journey took seven days, nineteen hours.

9. Amy Johnson.

10. First World War: Immelmann (German), Rickenbacker (American), Bishop (Canadian), Ball (British). Second World War: Cheshire, Gibson and Bader (British), Malan (South African).

11. (a) first to fly over the North Pole in 1926, and over the South Pole in 1929; (b) flew from London to Australia in 27 days; (c) made the first flight in Britain.

12. Colonel Charles Lindbergh.

Birthplaces

1. In which countries were these people born: (*a*) Adolf Hitler; (*b*) Christopher Columbus; (*c*) Karl Marx?

2. Who was the most famous person ever born at these places: (*a*) Stratford-on-Avon; (*b*) Lichfield; (*c*) Huntingdon; (*d*) Burnham Thorpe, Norfolk?

3. Which one of the following was *not* born in London? Samuel Pepys, Michael Faraday, Daniel Defoe, Lord Byron, Queen Anne, Francis Bacon, Winston Churchill.

4. Whose actual house of birth can be visited at: (*a*) Portsmouth; (*b*) Sudbury, Suffolk; (*c*) Alloway, Ayrshire?

5. Who was born at: (*a*) Elstow, Beds.; (*b*) Domrémy, near Nancy, France; (*c*) East Knoyle, Wilts.; (*d*) 17, Bruton St., London?

6. Who was the last British king who was not born in Britain?

7. Which of these were not born in Britain: Hilaire Belloc, Thackeray, Kipling, Florence Nightingale, Gustav Holst, Frederick Delius?

8. Where was Beethoven born: Cologne, Bonn, Hanover, Osnabruck or Berlin?

9. In which countries were the following born: (*a*) Erasmus; (*b*) Confucius; (*c*) Leonardo da Vinci?

10. Who is the odd one out of these: Charles Chaplin, Bob Hope, Cary Grant, Stan Laurel, Buster Keaton?

11. Which two famous Elizabethan sailors were born in Devon?

12. Which of the houses in which the following were born still exist: Winston Churchill, Grace Darling, Horatio Nelson, Jane Austen, the Brontë sisters?

Birthplaces

1. (*a*) Austria;   (*b*) Italy;
   (*c*) Germany.

2. (*a*) Shakespeare;   (*b*) Dr. Johnson;
   (*c*) Oliver Cromwell;   (*d*) Nelson.

3. Winston Churchill.

4. (*a*) Dickens;   (*b*) Gainsborough;
   (*c*) Burns.

5. (*a*) John Bunyan;   (*b*) Joan of Arc;
   (*c*) Christopher Wren;   (*d*) Queen Elizabeth II.

6. George II was born in Germany.

7. Belloc, Thackeray, Kipling and Florence Nightingale.

8. Bonn.

9. (*a*) Holland;   (*b*) China;
   (*c*) Italy.

10. Buster Keaton. All the others were born in England.

11. Sir Francis Drake and Sir Walter Raleigh.

12. Winston Churchill (Blenheim Palace), Grace Darling
    (at Bamburgh, Northumberland), the Brontë sisters (at
    Thornton, Yorkshire).

Burial Places

1. Where are these people buried: (*a*) Lord Nelson; (*b*) Dr. Johnson; (*c*) Napoleon Bonaparte?

2. Which two famous English poets are buried in Rome?

3. Name two of the four English kings buried in France and the one buried in Germany.

4. Which famous Englishmen are buried in these villages: (*a*) Bladon, Oxford; (*b*) Moreton, Dorset.

5. Who was the last British king to be buried in Westminster Abbey? Where have most of them been buried since then?

6. Which famous Englishman is buried in: (*a*) Samoa; (*b*) the Antarctic?

7. In which cathedrals are the following buried: (*a*) King John; (*b*) Jane Austen; (*c*) Catherine of Aragon?

8. The following were buried in a country other than that in which they were born. Where are they buried? (*a*) Columbus; (*b*) Beethoven; (*c*) Leonardo da Vinci.

9. One of the most famous men in history was buried in a pauper's unmarked grave in Vienna in 1791. Who was he?

10. Which one of these is buried in England? Humphry Davy; John Ruskin; Henry Fielding; Joseph Priestley.

11. Which one of these is *not* buried in England? Karl Marx, Napoleon III of France, Empress Eugenie, Toulouse-Lautrec, Princess Pocahontas.

12. Which one of these Prime Ministers is buried in Westminster Abbey: Peel, Walpole, Disraeli, Gladstone, Wellington?

Burial Places

1. (*a*) St. Paul's Cathedral;   (*b*) Westminster Abbey;
   (*c*) Hôtel des Invalides, Paris.

2. Shelley and Keats.

3. William I, Henry II, Richard I and James II are buried
   in France and George I in Germany.

4. (*a*) Winston Churchill;   (*b*) T. E. Lawrence.

5. George II.   St. George's Chapel, Windsor.

6. (*a*) R. L. Stevenson;   (*b*) Captain Scott.

7. (*a*) Worcester;   (*b*) Winchester;
   (*c*) Peterborough.

8. (*a*) Dominican Republic;   (*b*) Vienna, Austria;
   (*c*) Amboise, France.

9. Mozart.

10. John Ruskin (Coniston).

11. Toulouse-Lautrec.

12. Gladstone.

Composers

1. What was the nationality of these composers: (*a*) Stravinsky; (*b*) Mozart; (*c*) Ravel; (*d*) Liszt; (*e*) Delius; (*f*) Chopin?

2. Who composed his first symphony at the age of eight, and later in life wrote three symphonies in forty days?

3. Name the son of a poor wheelwright who wrote 104 symphonies.

4. Who wrote the music for these operas: (*a*) *Fidelio*; (*b*) *Iolanthe*; (*c*) *The Bartered Bride*; (*d*) *William Tell*; (*e*) *Peter Grimes*; (*f*) *Der Rosenkavalier*?

5. Which composer: (*a*) became deaf in his prime; (*b*) took religious orders; (*c*) escaped arrest as a political revolutionary in 1848?

6. Who was William Byrd?

7. Who composed the music for *Oklahoma*?

8. What relationship was Wagner to Liszt?

9. Name two operas by Verdi.

10. What have Elgar, Delius and Holst in common?

11. Who composed these symphonies; (*a*) *Jupiter*; (*b*) *Manfred*; (*c*) *Italian*; (*d*) *Surprise*; (*e*) *Unfinished*; (*f*) *Pastoral*?

12. Which of the following *could* have met by virtue of being alive at the same period: Mozart, Beethoven, Brahms?

Composers

1. (*a*) Russian;   (*b*) Austrian;
   (*c*) French;   (*d*) Hungarian;
   (*e*) English;   (*f*) Polish.

2. Mozart.

3. Haydn.

4. (*a*) Beethoven;   (*b*) Sullivan;
   (*c*) Smetana;   (*d*) Rossini;
   (*e*) Britten;   (*f*) Richard Strauss.

5. (*a*) Beethoven;   (*b*) Liszt;
   (*c*) Wagner.

6. English composer of church and keyboard music and madrigals, famous in his day (1543–1623).

7. Richard Rodgers.

8. Wagner was the son-in-law of Liszt.

9. *Aida*; *La Traviata*; *Il Trovatore*; *Rigoletto*;

10. They were all English composers who died in the same year (1934).

11. (*a*) Mozart;   (*b*) Tchaikovsky;
    (*c*) Mendelssohn;   (*d*) Haydn;
    (*e*) Schubert;   (*f*) Beethoven.

12. Mozart could have met Beethoven. Brahms could not have met the other two.

Cricketers

1. Name the only cricketer ever to have played in more than 100 Test matches.

2. Who played in the greatest number of matches in the British county championship? Which county did he represent?

3. Which batsman scored most first-class runs: (*a*) in a season; (*b*) in his career; (*c*) in an innings?

4. Which bowler took most first-class wickets: (*a*) in a season; (*b*) in his career; (*c*) in a match?

5. Who was the only cricketer ever to: (*a*) score 2,000 runs and take 200 wickets in a season; (*b*) score 3,000 runs and take 100 wickets in a season?

6. Who has played in the most Test matches for: (*a*) Australia; (*b*) West Indies; (*c*) South Africa; (*d*) New Zealand; (*e*) India; (*f*) Pakistan?

7. Name the oldest and youngest players ever to appear in a Test match.

8. For which first-class counties did these players appear: (*a*) W. G. Grace; (*b*) J. B. Hobbs; (*c*) D. C. S. Compton?

9. Who has captained England the most times?

10. Which cricketers were known as: (*a*) 'The Croucher'; (*b*) 'The Don'; (*c*) 'The Doctor'; (*d*) 'The Demon'?

11. Who averaged 99·94 runs per innings in Test matches?

12. For which countries did these players appear: (*a*) M. P. Donnelly; (*b*) V. Merchant; (*c*) K. S. Ranjitsinhji; (*d*) F. M. Worrell; (*e*) V. Trumper; (*f*) D. J. McGlew?

Cricketers

1. M. C. Cowdrey of Kent and England.

2. Wilfred Rhodes appeared 763 times for Yorkshire between 1898 and 1930.

3. (a) D. C. S. Compton; 3,816 in 1947; (b) J. B. Hobbs; 61,237 between 1905 and 1934; (c) Hanif Mohammad; 499 for Karachi v. Bahawalpur in 1959.

4. (a) A. P. Freeman; 304 for Kent in 1928; (b) Wilfred Rhodes; 4,187 between 1898 and 1930; (c) J. C. Laker; 19 for 90 runs for England v. Australia, Old Trafford, 1956.

5. (a) G. H. Hirst of Yorkshire in 1906; 2,385 runs and 208 wickets; (b) J. H. Parks of Sussex in 1937; 3,003 and 101.

6. (a) R. N. Harvey; 79; (b) G. S. Sobers; 93; (c) J. H. Waite; 50; (d) J. R. Reid; 58; (e) P. Umrigar; 59; (f) Hanif Mohammad; 55.

7. Wilfred Rhodes, aged 52 for England v. W. Indies, 1930; Mushtaq Mohammad, aged 15, for Pakistan v. W. Indies, 1959.

8. (a) Gloucestershire;   (b) Surrey;
   (c) Middlesex.

9. P. B. H. May, 41 times.

10. (a) G. L. Jessop;   (b) D. G. Bradman;
    (c) W. G. Grace;   (d) F. R. Spofforth.

11. D. G. Bradman, in 52 Tests between 1928 and 1948.

12. (a) New Zealand;   (b) India;
    (c) England;   (d) West Indies;
    (e) Australia;   (f) South Africa.

Dates of Birth

1. These famous people were all born in the same decade of the nineteenth century. Which decade? Einstein, Rachmaninov, Schweitzer, Chesterton, Amundsen.

2. Arrange the following in chronological order of birth: Nelson, Byron, Beethoven, George Stephenson, Washington.

3. Two famous soldiers, later to oppose each other in battle, were both born in the year 1769. Who were they?

4. Give the dates of birth of the following to within 10 years: Shakespeare, Clive, Dr. Johnson, Oliver Cromwell.

5. Which one of the following was born first? Which one died first? Queen Victoria, Gladstone, Disraeli, Dickens.

6. Which one of these is the odd one out, and why? Noel Coward, J. B. Priestley, William Walton, Aldous Huxley.

7. Give these famous people their correct year of birth from the dates given: Michelangelo, Henry V, Elizabeth I, Marco Polo, Joan of Arc: 1254, 1387, 1412, 1475, 1533.

8. When was Jesus Christ born? When was He crucified?

9. What was the date of birth of Henry VIII: 1481, 1491, 1501 or 1511?

10. Which one of these was born in the reign of Queen Victoria? Thomas Hardy, George Meredith, George Eliot, Lewis Carroll.

11. Which one of these lived to the greatest age? Queen Victoria, Michelangelo, George Bernard Shaw, Picasso.

12. Arrange the following in chronological order of birth: Brahms, Rossini, Tchaikovsky, Mendelssohn.

Dates of Birth

1. They were born in 1879, 1873, 1875, 1874 and 1872 respectively.

2. Washington 1732; Nelson 1758; Beethoven 1770; George Stephenson 1781; Byron 1788.

3. Wellington and Napoleon Bonaparte.

4. Shakespeare 1564; Clive 1725; Dr. Johnson 1709; Oliver Cromwell 1599.

5. Disraeli was born first (1804), and Dickens died first (1870).

6. William Walton was born in the twentieth century (1902), the others in the nineteenth.

7. Michelangelo 1475; Henry V 1387; Elizabeth I 1533; Marco Polo 1254; Joan of Arc 1412.

8. He was born about the year 6 B.C. and died about 29 A.D.

9. 1491.

10. Thomas Hardy (1840).

11. George Bernard Shaw (94).

12. Rossini 1792; Mendelssohn 1809; Brahms 1833; Tchaikovsky 1840.

Dramatists

1. Who wrote these plays: (*a*) *The Rivals* (1775); (*b*) *Patience* (1881); (*c*) *The Doctor's Dilemma* (1906); (*d*) *The Caretaker* (1960)?

2. Who achieved sudden fame with his first play, *Journey's End*, in 1928?

3. Which London theatre, built in 1599, became famous for the presentation of Shakespeare's plays?

4. Which playwright was at one time music critic of the *Star*?

5. What nationality were the following: Chekhov, Ibsen, Gorky, Gogol?

6. Who wrote these famous plays: (*a*) *The Way of the World*; (*b*) *She Stoops to Conquer*; (*c*) *The School for Scandal*; (*d*) *Pygmalion*?

7. What have these in common: Greene, Peele, Webster, Marlowe, Kyd, Ford?

8. All the following except one specialized in comedy or satire. Which one did not? Feydeau, Molière, Shaw, Ibsen, Ionesco, Wilde.

9. A. A. Milne's *Toad of Toad Hall* is based on which famous children's book?

10. Which play by Agatha Christie has recorded more performances than any in the history of the British theatre?

11. Who wrote these ancient classical plays: (*a*) *The Frogs*; (*b*) *Oedipus Rex*; (*c*) *Electra*?

12. What other profession was followed by W. S. Gilbert?

Dramatists

1. (*a*) Sheridan;   (*b*) W. S. Gilbert;
   (*c*) G. B. Shaw;   (*d*) Pinter.

2. R. C. Sherriff.

3. The Globe.

4. George Bernard Shaw.

5. All were Russian except Ibsen, who was Norwegian.

6. (*a*) Congreve;   (*b*) Goldsmith;
   (*c*) Sheridan;   (*d*) G. B. Shaw.

7. They were all Elizabethan or Jacobean dramatists.

8. Ibsen.

9. *The Wind in the Willows* by Kenneth Grahame.

10. *The Mousetrap.*

11. (*a*) Aristophanes;   (*b*) Sophocles;
   (*c*) Euripides.

12. Barrister of the Inner Temple.

Eighteenth-Century People

1. Of whom was it said that he 'wrote the best play in the English language and made the best speech ever heard in Parliament'?

2. Who was Robespierre (1758–94)? What was his fate?

3. What is the connection between Sir Hans Sloane and the British Museum?

4. What did Robert Harley, 1st Earl of Oxford, establish in 1711 which 'burst' in 1720 bringing ruin to many people?

5. Who in 1755 wrote the first of one hundred and four?

6. Who was John Wilkes (1727–97)?

7. Who wrote his first novel at the age of 59 after being at various times a hosiery-factor, a government agent and a journalist?

8. His real name was Francois Marie Arouet. He was the greatest French writer of the century. Who was he?

9. In what field were these men famous: (a) Carolus Linnaeus; (b) Tobias Smollett; (c) George Romney; (d) Alessandro Scarlatti?

10. Which famous actor was a pupil of Samuel Johnson?

11. Which famous composer was born on 27th January 1756?

12. Complete the following:
    (a) Samuel .... (1689–1761), novelist;
    (b) Bishop George .... (1685–1753), philosopher;
    (c) Edward .... (1749–1823), physician;
    (d) Matthew .... (1728–1809), engineer.

Eighteenth-Century People

1. R. B. Sheridan. The play was *The School for Scandal*, and the speech was on the impeachment of Warren Hastings.

2. French revolutionary leader, one of the founders of the Jacobins. He was guillotined by his more moderate associates.

3. On his death his collection of books and specimens formed the nucleus of the British Museum.

4. The South Sea Company, known as the 'South Sea bubble'.

5. Franz Joseph Haydn – 104 symphonies.

6. A Member of Parliament, political reformer and Lord Mayor of London, whose zeal for reform and individual liberty earned him the nickname of 'Liberty' Wilkes.

7. Daniel Defoe with *Robinson Crusoe*.

8. Voltaire.

9. (*a*) Swedish botanist;   (*b*) Scottish novelist;
   (*c*) English painter;   (*d*) Italian composer.

10. David Garrick.

11. Mozart.

12. (*a*) Richardson;   (*b*) Berkeley;
    (*c*) Jenner;   (*d*) Boulton.

Explorers

1. Where exactly did Columbus land after his epic journey across the Atlantic in 1492?

2. (*a*) Who was the first man to circumnavigate the earth? (*b*) Who was the first Englishman to do so? (*c*) Who was the first American to do so?

3. Name the sixteenth-century Spanish conqueror of Mexico, and also the Spanish conqueror of Peru.

4. (*a*) Which European first rounded the Cape of Good Hope? (*b*) Who first rounded Cape Horn? (*c*) Who discovered the sea route to India via S. Africa?

5. (*a*) Who was the first European to visit the east coast of Australia? (*b*) Who was the first to visit New Zealand?

6. Who first reached the South Pole, and who reached it a month later? Who had been to within 100 miles of it two years previously?

7. Who first reached the North Pole?

8. (*a*) Who was the first Englishman to cross Africa south of the Equator? (*b*) Who was the first to cross North America? (*c*) Who was the first to reach Japan?

9. Who discovered Lake Victoria?

10. Which explorers sailed on these ships: (*a*) *Trinidad*; (*b*) *Golden Hind*; (*c*) *Santa Maria*; (*d*) *Endeavour*; (*e*) *Fram*?

11. Give the location of the places to which the following gave their names: (*a*) Barents; (*b*) Bering; (*c*) Hudson.

12. Marco Polo was a native of which city?

Explorers

1. Most probably at Guanahani Island, now San Salvador or Watling Island, in the Bahamas.

2. (*a*) Sebastian del Cano, 1519–22. He took over the leadership of Magellan's expedition when the latter was killed; (*b*) Sir Francis Drake, 1577–80; (*c*) Robert Gray, 1787–89.

3. Hernando Cortès, and Francisco Pizarro.

4. (*a*) Bartholomew Diaz, 1487–88; (*b*) Sir Francis Drake, 1578; (*c*) Vasco de Gama, 1497–98.

5. (*a*) Captain Cook, 1770; (*b*) Abel Tasman, 1642.

6. First was Roald Amundsen, followed by Captain Scott. Ernest Shackleton had been within 100 miles.

7. Commander Robert Peary, 1909.

8. (*a*) David Livingstone, 1854–56; (*b*) Alexander Mackenzie, 1793; (*c*) William Adams, 1600.

9. J. H. Speke, 1858.

10. (*a*) Magellan; (*c*) Drake; (*c*) Columbus; (*d*) Captain Cook (first voyage); (*e*) Nansen.

11. (*a*) Barents Sea – in the Arctic ocean north of Norway and Russia; (*b*) Bering Straits – between Alaska and Russia; (*c*) Hudson's Bay – Canada.

12. Venice, Italy.

Fact or Fiction?

1. 'The boy stood on the burning deck ...' Was Mrs. Hemans' character based on fact or fiction?

2. Was there ever a person by the name of Robinson Crusoe?

3. Were: (*a*) Dick Turpin and (*b*) Dick Whittington real people?

4. What was the name of the fictitious knight portrayed by Addison and Steele in the *Spectator*?

5. Who was 'Bonnie Prince Charlie'?

6. Were: (*a*) Annie Laurie and (*b*) Lady Godiva real people?

7. Who was 'Rob Roy'?

8. Were these real people: (*a*) Casanova; (*b*) Don Juan; (*c*) Robin Hood?

9. What was the name of the outlaw who held the Isle of Ely against the attacks of the Normans?

10. What were the names of the legendary twins who were brought up by wolves and supposedly founded Rome?

11. Which of these was a real person: Tom Sawyer, Roger Tichborne, Reuben Starkadder, Arthur Kipps, Felix Holt, Philip Trent?

12. Were: (*a*) Captain Kidd and (*b*) Captain Hook real pirates?

Fact or Fiction?

1. Fact. His name was Giacomo Casabianca; his father was captain of the French ship *Orient* at the battle of the Nile; both he and his father died on the ship.

2. No, but Defoe's story was based on the real adventures of Alexander Selkirk who spent four years alone on one of the islands of Juan Fernandez.

3. Yes.

4. Sir Roger de Coverley.

5. Charles Edward Stuart, the 'Young Pretender'.

6. Yes. Annie Laurie was the daughter of Sir Robert Laurie of Maxwelltown, and Lady Godiva was the wife of Leofric, Earl of Mercia.

7. Robert MacGregor (1671–1734), a Scottish outlaw.

8. (*a*) Yes; (*b*) No; (*c*) No.

9. Hereward the Wake.

10. Romulus and Remus.

11. Roger Tichborne.

12. (*a*) Yes; (*b*) No – a character in Barrie's *Peter Pan*.

Famous Americans

1. Who were: (*a*) 'Buffalo Bill'; (*b*) 'Calamity Jane'; (*c*) 'Davy Crockett'?

2. Who were P. T. Barnum and Charles S. Stratton, and how were they connected?

3. Who was: (*a*) Thomas ('Stonewall') Jackson; (*b*) Andrew Jackson?

4. Which one of these is *not* an American citizen? Charles Chaplin, Orson Welles, Frank Sinatra, Elvis Presley.

5. Which one of these was actually born in the United States: Bob Hope, Cary Grant, Oliver Hardy, Stan Laurel, Boris Karloff, Ray Milland?

6. Name the Red Indian princess who married an Englishman, went to England in 1616 and died there.

7. What have these in common: J. D. Rockefeller, Henry Ford, Dale Carnegie, J. J. Astor, C. Vanderbilt?

8. What have these in common: Martin van Buren, Grover Cleveland, James Knox Polk, Millard Fillmore?

9. Who was the first American to be awarded the Nobel prize for literature?

10. Who were the opposing generals at the battle of Appomattox in 1865?

11. Who was: (*a*) the first Postmaster of the U.S.A.; (*b*) the first Ambassador to Britain?

12. Who wrote: (*a*) *The Song of Hiawatha*; (*b*) *Walden; or Life in the Woods*; (*c*) *The Adventures of Tom Sawyer*; (*d*) *The Murders in the Rue Morgue*?

Famous Americans

1. (*a*) William F. Cody, frontiersman and showman; (*b*) Martha Jane Burke, Army scout and frontierswoman; (*c*) frontiersman and Army colonel from Tennessee.

2. Barnum was a showman and owner of a travelling circus, and at one time employed Stratton, who was better known as 'General Tom Thumb', the famous dwarf.

3. (*a*) Confederate general in the Civil War; (*b*) President of the United States 1829–37.

4. Charles Chaplin.

5. Oliver Hardy.

6. Pocahontas (1595–1617).

7. They were all millionaires.

8. They were all Presidents of the United States.

9. Sinclair Lewis in 1930.

10. Robert E. Lee and Ulysses S. Grant.

11. (*a*) Benjamin Franklin;   (*b*) John Adams.

12. (*a*) Henry Wadsworth Longfellow; (*b*) Henry David Thoreau; (*c*) Mark Twain; (*d*) Edgar Allan Poe.

Famous Children

1. Who were the 'Princes in the Tower'?

2. What have Shirley Temple, Jackie Cooper and Jackie Coogan in common?

3. Who had a series of visions at Lourdes, France, in 1858 and what was the result?

4. Who was Alice Liddell?

5. Who started composing at the age of five and toured Europe and played before royalty at the age of six?

6. Who wrote a 'compendium of universal history' at the age of seven?

7. Who wrote a best-selling novel at the age of nine?

8. Edmund Waller was only 15 in 1621 when he was elected to what?

9. Can you give the year of birth of two of the Queen's four children?

10. Who was the father of Peter Scott the naturalist?

11 Who became King of England at the age of: (*a*) 14; (*b*) 10; (*c*) 9 months; (*d*) 13; (*e*) 9?

12. The father was a Prime Minister of Great Britain, the son a famous man of letters and biographer. Who were they?

Famous Children

1. Edward V, son of Edward IV, and his brother Richard, Duke of York.

2. All child film stars of the nineteen-thirties.

3. St. Bernadette of Lourdes (Marie-Bernarde Soubirous). Lourdes became a world-famous centre for pilgrims.

4. A young friend of Lewis Carroll for whom he wrote *Alice's Adventures in Wonderland*.

5. Mozart.

6. Thomas Babington Macaulay.

7. Daisy Ashford – *The Young Visiters*. It was not however published till many years after she wrote it – in 1919.

8. The House of Commons.

9. Charles 1948; Anne 1950; Andrew 1960; Edward 1964.

10. Captain Robert Scott, the Polar explorer.

11. (*a*) Edward III;   (*b*) Richard II;
    (*c*) Henry VI;   (*d*) Edward V;
    (*e*) Edward VI.

12. Sir Robert Walpole and Horace Walpole.

Famous Women

1. Name one of the first two women to have been made members of the Order of Merit.

2. Who were: (*a*) Grace Darling; (*b*) Edith Cavell; (*c*) Flora Macdonald?

3. Which Queen said 'Let them eat cake!'? Who were 'them'? How did 'they' get their revenge?

4. Who were Madame Du Barry and Madame Pompadour?

5. Who wrote these books: (*a*) *Little Women*; (*b*) *Little Lord Fauntleroy*; (*c*) *The Tale of Peter Rabbit*?

6. The following were the first women to become what? (*a*) Angelica Kauffman; (*b*) Elizabeth Garrett Anderson; (*c*) Mrs. Sirimawo Bandaranaike.

7. Who was Boadicea, or Boudicca? How did she die?

8. How did Jean Batten and Amelia Earheart achieve fame?

9. Which is the odd one out of these: Ella Wheeler Wilcox, Kate Greenaway, Christina Rossetti, Felicia Hemans?

10. What was the name of the most prominent English champion of women's suffrage in the early twentieth century?

11. Which Polish-born woman shared with her husband in 1903 the Nobel prize for physics?

12. Which of the Brontë sisters died first? Which of them married?

Famous Women

1. Florence Nightingale (1907) and Dorothy Hodgkin (1965).

2. (*a*) lighthouse-keeper's daughter who in 1838 helped to rescue the crew of the wrecked *Forfarshire*; (*b*) English nurse executed by the Germans in 1915; (*c*) Scotswoman who helped to save Prince Charles Edward after Culloden.

3. Marie Antoinette, wife of Louis XVI, when told that the poor people had no bread. She was executed on the guillotine in 1793.

4. Both mistresses of Louis XV of France.

5. (*a*) Louisa M. Alcott; (*b*) Frances Hodgson Burnett; (*c*) Beatrix Potter.

6. (*a*) first woman member of the Royal Academy; (*b*) first woman doctor and first woman mayor (of Aldeburgh); (*c*) first woman Prime Minister (of Ceylon).

7. Queen of the Iceni tribe in East Anglia in Roman times. She committed suicide after defeat by the Roman armies.

8. Jean Batten flew solo from England to Australia in 1934 and Amelia Earheart flew across the Atlantic in 1932.

9. Kate Greenaway was an artist and book illustrator and the others were poetesses.

10. Emmeline Pankhurst (1858–1928).

11. Marie Curie (1867–1934).

12. Emily died in 1848, Anne in 1849 and Charlotte in 1855. Charlotte was the only one to marry.

Film Stars

1. Who was known as: (a) 'the world's sweetheart'; (b) 'the "It" girl'?

2. Complete these famous pairs: (a) .... and Lou Costello; (b) .... and Oliver Hardy; (c) .... and Chesney Allen.

3. What were the stage-names of the three most famous Marx brothers? What were the names of the other two brothers?

4. What have the following in common: Boris Karloff, Bela Lugosi, Lon Chaney?

5. Who was the star of *The Jazz Singer*, the first successful talking feature film?

6. Which famous fictional characters were portrayed in films by: (a) Johnny Weissmuller; (b) Sean Connery?

7. Who was the star of these films: (a) *City Lights*; (b) *M*; (c) *Sunset Boulevard*; (d) *Dr. Dolittle*?

8. Of which film stars were these the real names: (a) Spangler Arlington Brough; (b) Marion Morrison; (c) Emmanuel Goldenberg; (d) Frances Gumm?

9. What do these have in common: Claude Rains; Boris Karloff; Charles Chaplin; Bob Hope?

10. Who were the stars of these films: (a) *The Blue Angel*; (b) *Dr. Zhivago*; (c) *Mrs. Miniver*; (d) *High Noon*?

11. Who directed these films: (a) *The Third Man*; (b) *Lawrence of Arabia*; (c) *The Battleship Potemkin*; (d) *Intolerance*?

12. In which country were these stars born: (a) Ramon Navarro; (b) George Sanders; (c) Greta Garbo; (d) Rudolph Valentino; (e) Marlene Dietrich; (f) Omar Sharif?

Film Stars

1. (*a*) Mary Pickford;   (*b*) Clara Bow.

2. (*a*) Bud Abbott;   (*b*) Stan Laurel;
   (*c*) Bud Flanagan.

3. Groucho, Chico and Harpo. Zeppo and Gummo.

4. They were all actors who starred in 'horror' films.

5. Al Jolson.

6. (*a*) Tarzan of the Apes;   (*b*) James Bond.

7. (*a*) Charles Chaplin;   (*b*) Peter Lorre;
   (*c*) Gloria Swanson;   (*d*) Rex Harrison.

8. (*a*) Robert Taylor;   (*b*) John Wayne;
   (*c*) Edward G. Robinson;   (*d*) Judy Garland.

9. They were all born in London.

10. (*a*) Marlene Dietrich and Emil Jannings; (*b*) Omar
    Sharif and Julie Christie; (*c*) Greer Garson and Walter
    Pidgeon; (*d*) Gary Cooper and Grace Kelly.

11. (*a*) Carol Reed;   (*b*) David Lean;
    (*c*) S. M. Eisenstein;   (*d*) D. W. Griffith.

12. (*a*) Mexico;   (*b*) Russia;
    (*c*) Sweden;   (*d*) Italy;
    (*e*) Germany;   (*f*) Egypt.

Footballers

(All questions are on Association football)

1. Who has gained the most International caps for England?

2. For which League clubs did these play: (*a*) Stanley Matthews; (*b*) Billy Meredith; (*c*) Billy Wright; (*d*) Tom Finney?

3. Who holds the record for scoring the highest number of goals in a Football League match?

4. For which clubs did Alf Ramsey play, and of which club did he become manager when he gave up playing?

5. Who has scored most goals in one English League season?

6. Who set up a record by scoring three goals in the 1966 World Cup Final?

7. For which countries did these players appear: (*a*) Eusebio; (*b*) Pele; (*c*) Puskas; (*d*) Di Stefano?

8. In F.A. Cup Finals: (*a*) who was the star of the 1953 Bolton–Blackpool game; (*b*) who played on with a broken neck in 1956; (*c*) who scored in 1938 with a penalty in the last minute of extra time?

9. What record was set by Jimmy Dickinson of Portsmouth?

10. Which countries did these represent: (*a*) George Best; (*b*) Denis Law; (*c*) George Cohen; (*d*) Ivor Allchurch; (*e*) Danny Blanchflower; (*f*) Alan Ball?

11. Which two brothers played for England in a World Cup Final?

12. What record is held by George Arthur Rowley?

Footballers

1. Bobby Moore – 108 caps.

2. (*a*) Stoke City and Blackpool; (*b*) Manchester City and Manchester United; (*c*) Wolverhampton Wanderers; (*d*) Preston North End.

3. Joe Payne, 10 for Luton Town v. Bristol Rovers in 1936.

4. Southampton and Tottenham Hotspur. Ipswich Town.

5. 'Dixie' Dean of Everton in 1927–8; 60 goals.

6. G. Hurst of West Ham United.

7. (*a*) Portugal;   (*b*) Brazil;
    (*c*) Hungary;   (*d*) Argentina.

8. (*a*) Stanley Matthews; (*b*) Bert Trautmann of Manchester City; (*c*) George Mutch of Preston North End.

9. He played in 764 games for Portsmouth between 1946 and 1965, the greatest number in football history.

10. (*a*) Northern Ireland;   (*b*) Scotland;
    (*c*) England;   (*d*) Wales;
    (*e*) Northern Ireland;   (*f*) England.

11. Jack and Bobby Charlton in 1966.

12. He has scored the record number of goals in English League football – 434 between 1946 and 1965.

Husbands and Wives

1. Who was the wife of: (a) Louis XVI; (b) Shakespeare?

2. Who was the 'official' wife of the Prince Regent, later George IV? Whom did he marry secretly?

3. Can you name all of the six wives of Henry VIII?

4. Who was the husband of: (a) Queen Victoria; (b) Queen Alexandra; (c) Queen Anne?

5. What have these in common: Michael Wilding, Mike Todd, Eddie Fisher, Richard Burton?

6. Name one of the three husbands of Mary, Queen of Scots.

7. Of which English kings were these the wives: (a) Caroline of Ansbach; (b) Catherine of Braganza; (c) Mary of Modena; (d) Eleanor of Aquitaine?

8. Who was the husband of: (a) Elizabeth Barrett; (b) Elizabeth Porter; (c) Elizabeth St. Michel?

9. Which of these *never* married: George Bernard Shaw, G. K. Chesterton, Anthony Trollope, W. M. Thackeray, Charles Lamb, Charles Dickens?

10. Were Byron and Shelley ever married? If so, to whom?

11. Who was the husband of: (a) Jane Welsh; (b) Sarah Jennings; (c) Clementine Hozier?

12. What relationship were Queen Victoria and Prince Albert before their marriage?

Husbands and Wives

1. (*a*) Marie Antoinette;   (*b*) Ann Hathaway.

2. Caroline of Brunswick. He secretly married Mrs. Fitzherbert in 1785.

3. Catherine of Aragon, Anne Boleyn, Jane Seymour, Anne of Cleves, Catherine Howard, Catherine Parr.

4. (*a*) Albert of Saxe-Coburg-Gotha; (*b*) King Edward VII; (*c*) Prince George of Denmark.

5. All were married to film star Elizabeth Taylor.

6. Earl of Bothwell, Earl of Darnley and the Dauphin of France.

7. (*a*) George II;   (*b*) Charles II;
   (*c*) James II;   (*d*) Henry II.

8. (*a*) Robert Browning;   (*b*) Samuel Johnson;
   (*c*) Samuel Pepys.

9. Charles Lamb.

10. Byron married Anne Milbanke, who left him after one year, and Shelley married first Harriet Westbrook and second Mary Wollstonecraft Godwin.

11. (*a*) Thomas Carlyle; (*b*) John Churchill, Duke of Marlborough; (*c*) Winston Churchill.

12. First cousins.

Inventors

1. What did each of the following invent for use in the spinning industry: (*a*) Richard Arkwright; (*b*) Samuel Crompton; (*c*) James Hargreaves?

2. Who invented these: (*a*) astronomical telescope; (*b*) radar; (*c*) wireless telegraph; (*d*) steam turbine; (*e*) telephone?

3. What did the following invent: (*a*) John Harrison; (*b*) Wm. Friese-Greene; (*c*) J. L. Macadam; (*d*) Jethro Tull?

4. Give the date and if possible the inventor of the first practical: (*a*) typewriter; (*b*) adding-machine; (*c*) safety-razor; (*d*) sewing-machine; (*e*) cash register.

5. Can you differentiate between the inventions of James Watt, Richard Trevithick, Thomas Newcomen and George Stephenson?

6. What was patented in 1836 by John Ericsson, a Swedish-born naval engineer?

7. What invention in 1934 by Percy Shaw has saved many thousands of lives on the road?

8. What was invented by: (*a*) Sir Charles Wheatstone in 1840; (*b*) Henry Greathead in 1789; (*c*) Edison in 1877?

9. Leonardo da Vinci (1452–1519) invented which of these: paddle-wheel, helicopter, parachute, mincing-machine, microscope, canal lock-gates?

10. Which famous American invented which safety device in 1752?

11. Archimedes (287–212 B.C.) was one of the earliest inventors. He is credited with the invention of which common object?

12. What invention of Johann Gutenberg was perhaps the most important in all history?

Inventors

1. (*a*) spinning frame;   (*b*) spinning 'mule';
   (*c*) spinning 'jenny'.

2. (*a*) Galileo, 1609; (*b*) Robert Watson-Watt, 1935; (*c*) Marconi, 1894; (*d*) Charles Parsons, 1884; (*e*) Alexander Graham Bell, 1876.

3. (*a*) chronometer, 1735; (*b*) cinematograph, 1889; (*c*) a method of road-surfacing, 1815; (*d*) agricultural drill, about 1701.

4. (*a*) C. Scholes, 1867;   (*b*) B. Pascal, 1642–44;
   (*c*) K. Gillette, 1901;   (*d*) Elias Howe, 1846;
   (*e*) J. Ritty, 1879.

5. Watt invented the modern high-pressure steam engine, Trevithick the first steam locomotive, Newcomen the atmospheric steam engine, and Stephenson developed the steam railway locomotive.

6. The screw propeller.

7. The 'cat's-eye' reflector.

8. (*a*) electric clock;   (*b*) lifeboat;
   (*c*) phonograph.

9. All except the microscope.

10. Benjamin Franklin invented the lightning conductor.

11. The screw.

12. He perfected the first printing press with movable type and on it printed the famous Gutenberg Bible.

Kings and Queens

1. Who was the only representative of the House of Saxe-Coburg-Gotha on the British throne?

2. Which sovereign enjoyed the longest reign on: (a) the British throne; (b) any European throne?

3. Three successive sovereigns of England had the same father. Who were they and who was the father?

4. Of the kings on the English or British throne since 1066 name: (a) three who were not married; (b) three who were not born in Britain.

5. Where are the burial places of: (a) William the Conqueror; (b) George I; (c) John; (d) Victoria; (e) Elizabeth I?

6. Which English king was: (a) murdered at Berkeley Castle; (b) beheaded in Whitehall; (c) killed at the battle of Bosworth?

7. Name the famous king of the Franks and emperor of the Romans who died in 814?

8. Of which famous ruling dynasty was Cleopatra a member?

9. Who was the last king of: (a) France; (b) Germany; (c) Italy?

10. Who was the last British king: (a) to lead his armies into battle; (b) to be unable to speak English?

11. Which British queen had 17 children, all of whom died at an early age?

12. (a) Which English queen remained unmarried? (b) Which English king and queen were crowned jointly?

47

Kings and Queens

1. King Edward VII.

2. (a) Queen Victoria – 63 years; (b) Louis XIV of France – 72 years.

3. Edward VI, Mary I and Elizabeth I, all children of Henry VIII.

4. (a) William II, Edward V, Edward VI. Edward VIII was unmarried while he was king; (b) William I, William II, Stephen, Henry II, Richard II, Edward IV, William III, George I, George II.

5. (a) Caen, Normandy; (b) Hanover, Germany; (c) Worcester Cathedral; (d) Frogmore, near Windsor; (e) Westminster Abbey.

6. (a) Edward II, 1327;   (b) Charles I, 1649;
   (c) Richard III, 1485.

7. Charlemagne.

8. The Ptolemies, Macedonian rulers of Egypt from 323 to 30 B.C.

9. (a) Napoleon III, deposed 1870, died 1873; (b) William II, abdicated 1918, died 1941; (c) Victor Emmanuel III, abdicated 1946, died 1947.

10. (a) George II, at Dettingen, Bavaria, 1743; (b) George I.

11. Queen Anne.

12. (a) Elizabeth I; (b) William III and Mary II, 1689.

Lords

1. Who was the first Duke of Bronte? Where is Bronte?

2. What was the family name of the Dukes of Norfolk?

3. What titles were taken by the following on elevation to the peerage: (*a*) Anthony Eden; (*b*) George Brown; (*c*) Max Aitken; (*d*) F. E. Smith?

4. Was Byron born into the aristocracy or was he created a peer? What was his full title?

5. What have the following in common: Duke of Monmouth (1649–1685); Duke of Northumberland (1665–1716); Duke of Richmond (1672–1723); Duke of St. Albans (1670–1726)?

6. Which of these Lords were at one time Prime Minister: 7th Earl of Shaftesbury, 2nd Earl of Liverpool, 4th Earl of Aberdeen, 5th Earl of Rosebery, Viscount Morley?

7. Which of these writers were given peerages: P. G. Wodehouse, C. P. Snow, Ted Willis?

8. Who was Lord Randolph Churchill (1849–95)?

9. Who was the first coloured man to be elevated to the British peerage?

10. Who was: (*a*) Lord John Russell; (*b*) the 3rd Earl Russell?

11. Which Lord was Queen Elizabeth I's chief secretary of state for forty years?

12. (*a*) Which poet was raised to the peerage in 1884? (*b*) Which Prime Minister was raised to the peerage in 1876? (*c*) Which historian and politician was raised in 1857?

Lords

1. Admiral Lord Nelson. Bronte is a town and province in Sicily; the title was granted by the King of Naples.

2. Fitzalan-Howard.

3. (*a*) Lord Avon;   (*b*) Lord George-Brown; (*c*) Lord Beaverbrook;   (*d*) Lord Birkenhead.

4. He succeeded to the title, as the 6th Baron Byron of Rochdale.

5. They were all illegitimate children of King Charles II.

6. Liverpool, Aberdeen and Rosebery.

7. C. P. Snow and Ted Willis.

8. The son of the 7th Duke of Marlborough, and father of Winston Churchill. He was at one time Chancellor of the Exchequer.

9. Lord Sinha of Raipur in 1919.

10. (*a*) British Prime Minister 1846–52 and 1865–6, who became the 1st Earl Russell; (*b*) Bertrand Russell, the celebrated philosopher and mathematician.

11. William Cecil, Lord Burghley (1520–98).

12. (*a*) Alfred Tennyson;   (*b*) Benjamin Disraeli; (*c*) Thomas Babington Macaulay.

Mathematicians and Astronomers

1. Why is the name Halley famous?

2. Who was John Napier?

3. Which famous Englishman, better known later as an architect, was formerly a Professor of Astronomy?

4. Who first stated: (a) that the Earth and planets orbit round the sun; (b) that all bodies fall with uniform acceleration; (c) the laws of planetary motion; (d) the law of gravitation?

5. Name the great seventeenth-century German philosopher and mathematician whose claim to have invented the differential calculus was disputed by Isaac Newton.

6. Who was: (a) Euclid; (b) Euler?

7. Who was the first Astronomer-Royal?

8. What nationality were the following: (a) Laplace; (b) Pythagoras; (c) Einstein; (d) Descartes?

9. Who was the German son of a bandmaster who was appointed private astronomer to George III?

10. Who was said to have jumped out of his bath and into the street on discovering a principle of hydrostatics?

11. Who was Tycho Brahe?

12. Why did Mercator become famous?

Mathematicians and Astronomers

1. Edmund Halley (1656–1742) was a famous astronomer who correctly predicted the return of the comet named after him.

2. The inventor of logarithms.

3. Sir Christopher Wren.

4. (a) Nikolaus Copernicus (1473–1543); (b) Galileo (1564–1642); (c) Johannes Kepler (1571–1630); (d) Isaac Newton (1642–1727).

5. Baron Gottfried Wilhelm von Leibniz (1646–1716).

6. (a) Euclid of Alexandria, a famous mathematician of about 300 B.C., wrote a treatise on geometry called the *Elements*; (b) Leonhard Euler of Switzerland (1707–83) was probably the most prolific mathematician of all time.

7. John Flamsteed was appointed in 1675 and held the office for 44 years.

8. (a) French; (b) Greek; (c) German, later American; (d) French.

9. Sir William Herschel (1738–1822).

10. Archimedes, the Greek mathematician.

11. A Danish astronomer (1564–1601) whose observations helped to confirm the theories of Copernicus.

12. He gave his name to the cylindrical map projection which is commonly used for navigational purposes.

Members of Parliament

1. In which year was Winston Churchill first elected to the House of Commons: 1890; 1895; 1900; 1905; 1910?

2. Which one of these was *never* a Member of Parliament: Edward Gibbon; Christopher Wren; Isaac Newton; Daniel Defoe; Robert Adam; Sir Walter Raleigh?

3. Who was a Member of Parliament for the longest period ever?

4. Who was the first woman: (*a*) elected to Parliament; (*b*) to take her seat in the House; (*c*) to become a Cabinet Minister?

5. Which British statesman once held all the great offices of state simultaneously?

6. (*a*) Which former Conservative M.P. became a Liberal Prime Minister? (*b*) Which former Liberal M.P. became a Conservative Prime Minister?

7. Who was the first Labour Member of Parliament?

8. To which political parties did these men belong: (*a*) Stanley Baldwin; (*b*) J. Ramsay MacDonald; (*c*) Herbert Asquith; (*d*) Henry Campbell-Bannerman?

9. Who was elected as the Member for these constituencies in 1974: (*a*) Huyton; (*b*) North Devon; (*c*) Sidcup?

10. For which constituencies were the following elected in October 1974: (*a*) Jo Grimond; (*b*) Enoch Powell; (*c*) Clement Freud?

11. When was the first coloured M.P. elected to the House?

12. Who were the famous 'Five Members'?

Members of Parliament

1. 1900.

2. Daniel Defoe.

3. Charles Villiers was a Member for 63 years, from 1835 to 1898, and was elected to the House 14 times.

4. (*a*) Countess Markiewicz in 1918; (*b*) Nancy Astor in 1919; (*c*) Margaret Bondfield, 1929–1931.

5. Wellington in 1834, while Peel was returning from abroad.

6. (*a*) Gladstone;   (*b*) Churchill.

7. Keir Hardie in 1892.

8. (*a*) Conservative;   (*b*) Labour;
   (*c*) Liberal;   (*d*) Liberal.

9. (*a*) Harold Wilson;   (*b*) Jeremy Thorpe;
   (*c*) Edward Heath.

10. (*a*) Orkney and Shetland;   (*b*) Down South;
    (*c*) Isle of Ely.

11. In 1892 Dadabhai Naoraji, an Indian, was elected as the Liberal Member for Central Finsbury.

12. Pym, Hampden, Hazlerigg, Holles and Strode. They were the five Members that Charles I attempted to arrest in the House of Commons on 4th of January 1642 but who had earlier fled to safety.

Mixed Bag

1. Who was the leader of the coup that deposed King Farouk of Egypt in 1952?

2. Who was the Franciscan monk who invented gunpowder and the magnifying glass in the thirteenth century?

3. Who were Chippendale, Sheraton and Hepplewhite?

4. Which Russian composer was: (*a*) a professor of chemistry; (*b*) a professor of military engineering?

5. What have these in common: Flinders Petrie, Howard Carter, Heinrich Schliemann, Austen Layard?

6. Who: (*a*) refused to be crowned king of England; (*b*) was ruler of England for less than a year, fled to the Continent and lived for another 53 years?

7. Who was the greatest orator of Roman times?

8. Who were Caractacus, Cunobelinus and Cogidubnus?

9. Who were: (*a*) Machiavelli; (*b*) Nostradamus; (*c*) Cagliostro?

10. What do these have in common: John Speed, Christopher Saxton, John Norden, Robert Morden?

11. What do these have in common: Jack Cade, Wat Tyler, Robert Kett?

12. Who were: (*a*) Rasputin; (*b*) Torquemada; (*c*) Paracelsus?

Mixed Bag

1. Colonel Gamal Abdel Nasser.

2. Roger Bacon.

3. All eighteenth-century furniture designers and cabinet-makers.

4. (*a*) Borodin; (*b*) Cui.

5. They were all archaeologists.

6. (*a*) Oliver Cromwell; (*b*) Richard Cromwell, son of Oliver Cromwell.

7. Marcus Tullius Cicero (106–43 B.C.)

8. They were all British tribal kings in Roman times.

9. (*a*) Florentine Renaissance diplomat and writer on political science; (*b*) sixteenth-century French astrologer and physician famous for his prophecies; (*c*) eighteenth-century charlatan and necromancer, imprisoned for freemasonry.

10. All English surveyors and mapmakers.

11. They were all leaders of peasant rebellions in England, Tyler in 1381, Cade in 1450 and Kett in 1549.

12. (*a*) Russian peasant monk who exercised a great and evil influence at Court; (*b*) Dominican prior, appointed head of the Spanish Inquisition in 1483, where he became famous for his cruelty; (*c*) early sixteenth-century Swiss physician and chemist who challenged contemporary medical practices.

Musicians

1. Which famous pianist and composer became Prime Minister of Poland?

2. Who was Antonio Stradivari (*c.* 1644–1737)?

3. What instruments do you associate with these musicians: (*a*) Artur Rubinstein; (*b*) Fritz Kreisler; (*c*) Dennis Brain; (*d*) Louis Armstrong?

4. Which one of these is or was *not* a famous pianist: Louis Kentner, Mark Hambourg, Leon Goossens, Fou T'Song?

5. What nationality were these conductors: (*a*) Toscanini; (*b*) Klemperer; (*c*) Barbirolli; (*d*) Ansermet?

6. Who was the conductor at the first Promenade Concert?

7. Name these conductors: (*a*) founded the London Philharmonic Orchestra; (*b*) studied as an engineer in Vienna.

8. What instruments do you associate with these musicians: (*a*) Larry Adler; (*b*) Yehudi Menuhin; (*c*) Pablo Casals; (*d*) Clifford Curzon?

9. Who is the odd one out of these: Geraldo, Ambrose, Henry Hall, Joe Loss, Glenn Miller?

10. What instruments are associated with these comedians: (*a*) Jack Benny; (*b*) Victor Borge; (*c*) Harpo Marx?

11. Which German-born pianist and conductor founded a famous orchestra in Manchester in 1857?

12. What instruments are associated with these: (*a*) Benny Goodman; (*b*) Liberace; (*c*) Jascha Heifetz; (*d*) Harry James?

Musicians

1. Ignace Jan Paderewski (1860–1941) became Prime Minister in 1919, but only for ten months.

2. He was a famous violin-maker of Cremona, Italy.

3. (a) piano;   (b) violin;
   (c) horn;   (d) trumpet.

4. Leon Goossens played the oboe.

5. (a) Italian;   (b) German;
   (c) English;   (d) Swiss.

6. Sir Henry Wood in 1895.

7. (a) Sir Thomas Beecham; (b) Herbert von Karajan.

8. (a) harmonica;   (b) violin;
   (c) cello;   (d) piano.

9. Glenn Miller was American, the others English.

10. (a) violin;   (b) piano;
    (c) harp.

11. Charles Hallé.

12. (a) clarinet;   (b) piano;
    (c) violin;   (d) trumpet.

Nineteenth-Century People

1. Who was 'Beau' Brummell and why was he so-called?

2. Who were John Bright and Richard Cobden and what great cause did they champion?

3. Who became German Chancellor in 1871 and was made a Prince?

4. On what occasion was a Prince Imperial of France killed whilst serving in the British Army?

5. Who were: (a) Sainte-Beuve; (b) Saint-Saëns?

6. Who were the 'Luddites'?

7. Why was George Loveless sentenced to seven years transportation to Australia in 1834?

8. For what are these people famous: (a) Karl Baedeker; (b) Thomas Barnardo; (c) Louis Braille; (d) Paul Reuter?

9. What have these men in common: William Butterfield, G. E. Street, J. L. Pearson, Charles Barry?

10. What did Count Cavour and Giuseppe Garibaldi achieve on 17 March 1861?

11. Which Russian author wrote: (a) *The Cherry Orchard*; (b) *The Brothers Karamazov*; (c) *The Government Inspector*?

12. What works of reference did the following originate: (a) Sir George Grove; (b) John Wisden; (c) Joseph Whitaker; (d) John Debrett?

Nineteenth-Century People

1. The son of Lord North's secretary, a dandy and wit who became famous for his extravagant mode of dress.

2. The leading members of the Anti-Corn Law League who as Members of Parliament agitated for Free Trade.

3. Otto von Bismarck-Schonhausen, usually known as Bismarck.

4. Prince Eugene, son of Napoleon III, was killed in the Zulu War of 1879.

5. (a) French literary critic (1804–69); (b) French composer (1835–1921).

6. Groups of working men (named after a certain 'Ned Ludd') who, fearing unemployment, destroyed textile machinery in the north of England from about 1811 to 1815.

7. He was the leader of the 'Tolpuddle Martyrs', who were convicted of administering illegal oaths in forming a trade union.

8. (a) German publisher of travel guide books; (b) founder of homes for destitute children; (c) inventor of a system of reading for the blind; (d) founder of the famous news agency, Reuters.

9. All famous Victorian architects.

10. They proclaimed the unification of Italy under King Victor Emmanuel II.

11. (a) Chekhov; (b) Dostoevsky; (c) Gogol.

12. (a) *Grove's Dictionary of Music and Musicians* (1879); (b) *Wisden's Cricketers' Almanack* (1864); (c) *Whitaker's Almanack* (1868); (d) *Debrett's Peerage* (1802).

Novelists

1. These novels were written by authors who wrote only one novel. Who were the authors? (*a*) *Wuthering Heights*; (*b*) *Savrola*; (*c*) *The Picture of Dorian Gray*; (*d*) *Rasselas*.
2. Who wrote these famous novels: (*a*) *Lorna Doone*; (*b*) *Moby Dick*; (*c*) *Don Quixote*; (*d*) *Frankenstein*; (*e*) *Tom Jones*?
3. Who created these detectives: (*a*) Hercule Poirot; (*b*) Sherlock Holmes; (*c*) Father Brown; (*d*) Lord Peter Wimsey?
4. Which of these novelists have been awarded the Nobel Prize: Rudyard Kipling; Pearl Buck; John Galsworthy; Arnold Bennett; Ernest Hemingway; John Buchan; John Steinbeck?
5. What other occupations had: (*a*) Anthony Trollope; (*b*) Sir Walter Scott; (*c*) Samuel Richardson; (*d*) Kenneth Grahame?
6. What have the following in common, and which were women: George Eliot; George Sand; George Orwell; George Birmingham?
7. Where were the following novelists born: (*a*) Karel Capek; (*b*) Jean-Jacques Rousseau; (*c*) J. Conrad?
8. These novels were all published anonymously. Who wrote them? (*a*) *Waverley*; (*b*) *Pamela*; (*c*) *Pride and Prejudice*.
9. Who created these characters: (*a*) Phileas Fogg; (*b*) Kimball O'Hara; (*c*) Mr. Bumble; (*d*) Becky Sharp; (*e*) Soames Forsyte?
10. What have these in common: (*a*) Kipling, Thackeray, Orwell; (*b*) Sterne, Swift, Kingsley?
11. Which European authors wrote these novels: (*a*) *Buddenbrooks*; (*b*) *War and Peace*; (*c*) *Madame Bovary*; (*d*) *Therese Racquin*?
12. Who wrote these American novels: (*a*) *The Red Badge of Courage*; (*b*) *Babbitt*; (*c*) *The Grapes of Wrath*; (*d*) *Gone with the Wind*?

Novelists

1. (*a*) Emily Brontë;   (*b*) Winston Churchill;
   (*c*) Oscar Wilde;   (*d*) Samuel Johnson.

2. (*a*) R. D. Blackmore;   (*b*) Herman Melville;
   (*c*) Miguel de Cervantes;   (*d*) Mary Shelley;
   (*e*) Henry Fielding.

3. (*a*) Agatha Christie;   (*b*) Arthur Conan Doyle;
   (*c*) G. K. Chesterton;   (*d*) Dorothy L. Sayers.

4. All except Arnold Bennett and John Buchan.

5. (*a*) Post Office official; (*b*) Clerk of Session and Sheriff of Selkirkshire; (*c*) printer; (*d*) Secretary of the Bank of England.

6. They are all pseudonyms of famous novelists. Two were women – George Eliot (Marian Evans) and George Sand (Amandine Dudevant, née Dupin).

7. (*a*) Czecho-Slovakia;   (*b*) Switzerland;
   (*c*) Poland.

8. (*a*) Sir Walter Scott;   (*b*) Samuel Richardson;
   (*c*) Jane Austen.

9. (*a*) Jules Verne;   (*b*) Rudyard Kipling;
   (*c*) Charles Dickens;   (*d*) W. M. Thackeray;
   (*e*) John Galsworthy.

10. (*a*) They were all born in India. (*b*) They were all clergymen.

11. (*a*) Thomas Mann;   (*b*) Tolstoy;
    (*c*) Gustave Flaubert;   (*d*) Emile Zola.

12. (*a*) Stephen Crane;   (*b*) Sinclair Lewis;
    (*c*) John Steinbeck;   (*d*) Margaret Mitchell.

Painters

1. Who painted these pictures: (*a*) *The Blue Boy*; (*b*) *The Boyhood of Raleigh*?

2. Which two Flemish painters were knighted by Charles I?

3. Who was the founder and leading member of the Impressionist school of painting?

4. Can you name the painter who: (*a*) invented the electric telegraph; (*b*) invented the helicopter and the parachute?

5. Who painted seventy pictures in the last seventy days of his life and shot himself at the age of 37?

6. Who were: (*a*) Tiziano Vecellio; (*b*) Domenikos Theotokopoulos; (*c*) R. van Rijn; (*d*) Antonio Canale?

7. Which son of a master gilder became a Spanish court painter for over thirty years?

8. Who was American-born, French-educated, English-domiciled, a dandy and wit, and sued Ruskin for libel?

9. Name two members of the Pre-Raphaelite school of painting.

10. For what type of paintings are the following famous: (*a*) Munnings; (*b*) Lely; (*c*) van Ruisdael; (*d*) Dali?

11. What were the Christian names of: (*a*) Turner; (*b*) Gainsborough; (*c*) Reynolds?

12. Who painted these pictures: (*a*) *The Cornfield*; (*b*) *The Fighting Temeraire* . . .; (*c*) *The Laughing Cavalier*?

Painters

1. (*a*) Gainsborough;   (*b*) Millais.

2. Peter Paul Rubens (1577–1640) in 1630 and Anthony van Dyck (1599–1641) in 1632.

3. Claude Monet (1840–1926).

4. (*a*) Samuel Morse (1791–1872); (*b*) Leonardo da Vinci (1452–1519).

5. Vincent van Gogh (1853–90).

6. (*a*) Titian;   (*b*) El Greco;
   (*c*) Rembrandt;   (*d*) Canaletto.

7. Goya.

8. James McNeil Whistler.

9. Millais, Holman Hunt, Burne-Jones, D. G. Rossetti and William Morris were the leading members.

10. (*a*) horses;   (*b*) portraits;
    (*c*) landscapes;   (*d*) surrealism.

11. (*a*) Joseph Mallord William; (*b*) Thomas; (*c*) Joshua.

12. (*a*) Constable;   (*b*) Turner;
    (*c*) Hals.

People in the Bible

1. Name the most famous son or sons of: (*a*) Adam; (*b*) Isaac and Rebecca; (*c*) David; (*d*) Zebedee.

2. Who was the oldest man in the Bible, and who were the next two oldest?

3. Who in the Bible symbolized: (*a*) lying; (*b*) wisdom; (*c*) patience?

4. Who was betrayed by: (*a*) Judas Iscariot; (*b*) Delilah?

5. What was the occupation of: (*a*) Luke; (*b*) Matthew?

6. (*a*) Who sold his birthright for a mess of pottage? (*b*) Who ordered the sun to stand still? (*c*) Who ordered the death of John the Baptist?

7. Name the three major prophets of the Old Testament.

8. Who was the unnamed female inhabitant of Sodom who suffered a most unusual death?

9. Who was cast into a den of lions? What happened to him? Who was the king who cast him in?

10. Name the wife of: (*a*) Abraham; (*b*) Boaz.

11. What was the relationship between: (*a*) Adam and Eve; (*b*) Ruth and Naomi; (*c*) Saul of Tarsus and Paul?

12. What were the names of the twelve apostles?

People in the Bible

1. (a) Cain and Abel;   (b) Esau and Jacob;
   (c) Solomon;   (d) James and John.

2. Methusaleh, 969 years, Jared (Methusaleh's grand-father), 962, and Noah, 950!

3. (a) Ananias;   (b) Solomon;
   (c) Job.

4. (a) Jesus;   (b) Samson.

5. (a) physician;   (b) tax-collector.

6. (a) Esau;   (b) Joshua;
   (c) Herod Antipas.

7. Isaiah, Ezekiel and Jeremiah.

8. Lot's wife, who turned into a pillar of salt.

9. Daniel. He prayed to the Lord, and the lions did not molest him. The king was Darius.

10. (a) Sarah;   (b) Ruth.

11. (a) husband and wife; (b) Ruth was Naomi's daughter-in-law; (c) the same person.

12. Simon Peter, Bartholomew, Andrew, James, John, Simon, Philip, Thomas, Matthew, Thaddeus, James the the son of Alpheus and Judas Iscariot.

Philosophers

1. Which famous Italian philosopher was a lens-maker by profession?

2. Name the Scottish Professor of Philosophy who became known as 'the father of political economy'. What was the title of his most famous book?

3. Which Roman emperor is better known as a philosopher?

4. Which is the odd one out of these: Kant, Hegel, Marx, Kierkegaard, Leibniz?

5. Which Greek philosopher formulated the principles of logic which have withstood the test of time for over 2,000 years?

6. Name these philosophers: (a) Lord Chancellor under James I, dismissed for corruption; (b) succeeded to an Earldom, awarded the Order of Merit; (c) born in Germany, died in England, wrote *Das Kapital*.

7. Who originated the idea of 'Utilitarianism', and who was its leading nineteenth-century exponent?

8. Who wrote: (a) *Essay Concerning Human Understanding*; (b) *Discourse on Method*; (c) *Critique of Pure Reason*?

9. Plato, Socrates and Aristotle were famous philosophers. Who was the pupil of whom?

10. Which Greek philosopher was said to have lived in a tub?

11. Who founded these philosophies: (a) Cynicism; (b) Stoicism?

12. Who was St. Thomas Aquinas?

Philosophers

1. Spinoza (1632–1677).

2. Adam Smith (1723–1790). *Inquiry into the Nature and Causes of the Wealth of Nations* (1776).

3. Marcus Aurelius Antoninus (121–180).

4. Kierkegaard was Danish. All the others were German.

5. Aristotle (384–322 B.C.).

6. (*a*) Francis Bacon;   (*b*) Bertrand Russell;
   (*c*) Karl Marx.

7. 'Utilitarianism', the theory of the greatest good of the greatest number, was originated by Jeremy Bentham (1748–1832), and its leading exponent was John Stuart Mill (1806–73).

8. (*a*) John Locke;   (*b*) Descartes;
   (*c*) Kant.

9. Plato was the pupil of Socrates, and Aristotle was the pupil of Plato.

10. Diogenes.

11. (*a*) Diogenes;   (*b*) Zeno of Citiam.

12. An Italian philosopher (1225–74) who established the official philosophy of the Roman Catholic Church.

Places Named After People

1. (a) Which American state is named after a President?
   (b) Which American city is named after a British Prime Minister?

2. Who gave their names to these places: (a) Bolivia; (b) Tasmania; (c) Rhodesia?

3. Name the cities named after: (a) the wife of William IV; (in Australia); (b) Alexander the Great (in Egypt).

4. Which Canadian province is named after a member of British royalty?

5. These London streets were named after certain people. Can you say who they were? (a) Savile Row; (b) Harley Street; (c) Regent Street.

6. After whom are these mountains named: (a) McKinley; (b) Everest?

7. Name these Russian cities named after famous people: (a) scene of prolonged battle in 1942–3, now re-named Volgograd; (b) formerly called St. Petersburg and Petrograd; (c) formerly called Nijni Novgorod.

8. After whom are these American states named: (a) Pennsylvania; (b) Virginia; (c) Maryland; (d) Louisiana?

9. After whom was the continent of America named?

10. Name the cities named after: (a) a British Prime Minister (in New Zealand); (b) an American President (in U.S.A.).

11. Which Norfolk man gave his name to the chief port of Canada?

12. Name a new town in the west Midlands named after a famous engineer.

Places Named After People

1. (a) Washington;   (b) Pittsburgh.

2. (a) Simon Bolivar;   (b) Abel Tasman;
   (c) Cecil Rhodes.

3. (a) Adelaide;   (b) Alexandria.

4. Alberta – Princess Louise Alberta, daughter of Queen Victoria.

5. (a) Dorothy Savile, wife of the third Earl of Burlington, who built it about 1735; (b) Robert Harley, first Earl of Oxford; (c) the Regent, later George IV.

6. (a) William McKinley, President of U.S.A.; (b) Sir George Everest, Surveyor-General of India.

7. (a) Stalingrad;   (b) Leningrad;
   (c) Gorky.

8. (a) William Penn and his father, Admiral Penn; (b) Elizabeth I, the 'Virgin' Queen; (c) Mary, wife of Charles I; (d) Louis XIV of France.

9. Amerigo Vespucci (1452–1512).

10. (a) Wellington;   (b) Washington.

11. George Vancouver (1758–98).

12. Telford.

Questions

Poets

1. Which famous poet was Latin Secretary to Oliver Cromwell?

2. Who was the first poet to be buried in Poets' Corner in Westminster Abbey?

3. Who was Virgil? What was his most famous work?

4. Who was the first Poet Laureate?

5. Which two of these held the office of Poet Laureate: Shakespeare, Milton, Byron, Shelley, Wordsworth, Browning, Tennyson, Kipling?

6. Who wrote these 'Odes': (a) *To Duty*; (b) *To a Nightingale*; (c) *To the West Wind*?

7. Who is the odd one out of these: Browning, Burns, Tennyson, Matthew Arnold?

8. Who wrote: (a) *Childe Harold's Pilgrimage*; (b) *The Ring and the Book*; (c) *Paradise Lost*; (d) *The Ancient Mariner*; (e) *Idylls of the King*; (f) *Intimations of Immortality*?

9. What were the Christian names of: (a) Byron; (b) Shelley; (c) Tennyson; (d) Coleridge?

10. Tennyson wrote a famous poem – *In Memoriam A.H.H.* Who was A.H.H.?

11. Thomas Gray's famous *Elegy written in a Country Churchyard* refers to which churchyard?

12. Who wrote these famous lines: (a) If I should die, think only this of me . . .; (b) The curfew tolls the knell of parting day . . .; (c) Water, water, everywhere. Nor any drop to drink . . .?

Poets

1. John Milton.

2. Geoffrey Chaucer in 1400.

3. Publius Vergilius Maro (70–19 B.C.), probably the greatest of all Roman poets, wrote the *Aeneid*.

4. John Dryden, in 1670.

5. Wordsworth and Tennyson.

6. (*a*) Wordsworth;   (*b*) Keats;
   (*c*) Shelley.

7. Burns lived in the eighteenth century, the others in the nineteenth. He was also the only Scotsman.

8. (*a*) Byron;   (*b*) Browning;
   (*c*) Milton;   (*d*) Coleridge;
   (*e*) Tennyson;   (*f*) Wordsworth.

9. (*a*) George Gordon; (*b*) Percy Bysshe;
   (*c*) Alfred;   (*d*) Samuel Taylor.

10. Arthur Henry Hallam (1811–33), a close friend.

11. Stoke Poges, Bucks.

12. (*a*) Rupert Brooke; (*b*) Thomas Gray;
    (*c*) Samuel Taylor Coleridge.

Presidents

1. Which father and son both became President of the United States?

2. How many Presidents of the United States were assassinated between 1865 and 1965?

3. Theodore R. Roosevelt and Franklin D. Roosevelt were Presidents of the United States. Were they related?

4. Who was President of France: (*a*) at the outbreak of war in 1939; (*b*) for the ten years 1959–69?

5. Who was the first President of the United States? For how long did he serve?

6. Franklin D. Roosevelt, Harry S. Truman, John F. Kennedy, Lyndon B. Johnson, Richard M. Nixon, Gerald Ford. Name the missing President from this list.

7. Who was the first President of the Royal Academy?

8. Which American President died of pneumonia after only one month in office?

9. Who was the first President of the French Republic?

10. Which United States Presidents were awarded the Nobel prize?

11. Which United States President was in office: (*a*) almost throughout the American Civil War; (*b*) throughout the 1914–18 War; (*c*) for most of the 1939–45 War?

12. Who became President of Eire forty years after being sentenced to life imprisonment?

Presidents

1. John Adams (1735–1826) – President 1797–1801, and John Quincy Adams (1767–1848) – President 1825–29.

2. Four – Lincoln (1865), Garfield (1881), McKinley (1901), and Kennedy (1963).

3. Yes, they were distant cousins.

4. (*a*) Albert Lebrun;   (*b*) Charles de Gaulle.

5. George Washington. 8 years (1789–97).

6. Dwight D. Eisenhower, who succeeded Truman.

7. Sir Joshua Reynolds in 1768.

8. William Henry Harrison in 1841.

9. Louis Napoleon in 1848.

10. Theodore Roosevelt in 1906 and Woodrow Wilson in 1919.

11. (*a*) Abraham Lincoln;   (*b*) Woodrow Wilson;
    (*c*) Franklin D. Roosevelt.

12. Eamon de Valera in 1959.

Prime Ministers

1. Which British Prime Minister held office for the longest continuous period?

2. Who were the oldest and youngest British Prime Ministers?

3. Who were the British Prime Ministers at the accession of Queen Victoria and at her death?

4. Name all the British Prime Ministers: (a) between 1918 and 1939; (b) between 1945 and 1973.

5. Which British Prime Ministers represented these places: (a) Bewdley; (b) Warwick and Leamington; (c) Epping; (d) Caernarvon Boroughs; (e) Tamworth; (f) East Fife?

6. Who was the first Prime Minister to be recognized as such? Who was the first to be officially recognized?

7. Which British Prime Minister was assassinated?

8. Who was British Prime Minister at the time of: (a) the Indian Mutiny; (b) Waterloo; (c) the General Strike of 1926; (d) the Boer War; (e) the Festival of Britain?

9. (a) Who was the last British Prime Minister to sit in the House of Lords? (b) Who was the last Liberal Prime Minister? (c) Who was the first Labour Prime Minister?

10. Which of these were *never* Prime Minister: Burke, Fox, Goderich, Joseph Chamberlain, Wellington, Gaitskell, Bonar Law, Canning?

11. During both World Wars the British Prime Minister at the time was forced to resign. Who were they?

12. At the outbreak of war in 1939 who was Prime Minister of: (a) South Africa; (b) Canada; (c) Australia?

Prime Ministers

1. Sir Robert Walpole, for nearly 21 years from 1721 to 1742.

2. Gladstone was 84 when he retired in 1894, and Pitt the Younger was only 24 when he took office in 1783.

3. Viscount Melbourne and the Marquis of Salisbury.

4. (*a*) Lloyd-George, Bonar Law, Baldwin, MacDonald, Chamberlain; (*b*) Attlee, Churchill, Eden, Macmillan, Douglas-Home, Wilson, Heath.

5. (*a*) Baldwin;　　　　　(*b*) Eden;
   (*c*) Churchill;　　　　(*d*) Lloyd-George;
   (*e*) Peel;　　　　　　(*f*) Asquith.

6. Sir Robert Walpole, and Sir Henry Campbell-Bannerman (in 1905).

7. Spencer Perceval, in 1812, in the lobby of the old Houses of Parliament.

8. (*a*) Palmerston; (*b*) the Earl of Liverpool; (*c*) Baldwin; (*d*) the Marquis of Salisbury; (*e*) Attlee.

9. (*a*) the Marquis of Salisbury, 1902; (*b*) David Lloyd-George, 1922; (*c*) J. Ramsay MacDonald, 1924.

10. Burke, Fox, Joseph Chamberlain and Gaitskell.

11. Chamberlain in 1940 and Asquith in 1916.

12. (*a*) General James Hertzog; (*b*) Mackenzie King; (*c*) Robert G. Menzies.

Pseudonyms and Nicknames

1. Who were: (*a*) Joseph Dzhugashvili; (*b*) Lev Davidovich Bronstein; (*c*) Vladimir Ilich Ulyanov?

2. Who wrote under these pseudonyms: (*a*) 'Q'; (*b*) Michael Angelo Titmarsh; (*c*) Artemus Ward?

3. What were the pseudonyms of the Brontë sisters?

4. Who was known as: (*a*) 'The Hammer of the Scots'; (*b*) 'Tumbledown Dick'; (*c*) 'The Sea-green Incorruptible'?

5. Who were: (*a*) Francois Marie Arouet; (*b*) Jacques Thibault; (*c*) Joseph Korzeniowski?

6. What name that became world-famous was adopted by Margarete MacLeod, a Dutch spy of the 1914–18 War?

7. Who were known as: (*a*) 'The Little Corporal'; (*b*) 'The Iron Chancellor'; (*c*) 'The Young Pretender'; (*d*) 'The Wisest Fool in Christendom'?

8. What names were adopted by: (*a*) John Henry Brodribb; (*b*) Josip Broz; (*c*) Daniel Kominski?

9. Which famous American writer adopted a riverboat term for his pen-name?

10. Complete the following: (*a*) Ivan the ....; (*b*) Ethelred the ....; (*c*) Suleiman the ....

11. Who conducted a lengthy correspondence under the pseudonyms of 'Mrs. Morley' and 'Mrs. Freeman'?

12. Who was: (*a*) 'Boz'; (*b*) 'Phiz'?

Pseudonyms and Nicknames

1. (*a*) Joseph Stalin;   (*b*) Leon Trotsky;
   (*c*) Lenin.

2. (*a*) Sir Arthur Quiller-Couch; (*b*) W. M. Thackeray; (*c*)
   Charles Farrar Browne.

3. Charlotte Brontë – Currer Bell; Emily Brontë – Ellis
   Bell; Anne Brontë – Acton Bell.

4. (*a*) Edward I;   (*b*) Richard Cromwell;
   (*c*) Robespierre.

5. (*a*) Voltaire;   (*b*) Anatole France;
   (*c*) Joseph Conrad.

6. Mata Hari.

7. (*a*) Napoleon Bonaparte; (*b*) Bismarck; (*c*) Charles
   Edward Stuart ('Bonnie Prince Charlie'); (*d*) James I.

8. (*a*) Henry Irving;   (*b*) Tito;
   (*c*) Danny Kaye.

9. Mark Twain, which means literally 'exactly two
   fathoms' and was a cry used to warn the navigator of
   shallow areas.

10. (*a*) Terrible;   (*b*) Unready;
    (*c*) Magnificent.

11. Queen Anne and Sarah Churchill, Duchess of Marl-
    borough.

12. (*a*) Charles Dickens; (*b*) Hablot K. Browne, who
    illustrated many of Dickens's novels.

Record-Breakers

1. How did a painting by Velazquez set a record?

2. Which of these authors wrote 564 books in just over forty years: Georges Simenon, John Creasey, Raymond Chandler, Edgar Wallace?

3. Where did Henry Peter Brougham have a lot to say on 7th February 1828?

4. Who in 1685 sentenced 330 people to be hanged and 841 to be transported?

5. What record is held by Nobel prize-winner Dr. Linus Pauling?

6. Who has won the most 'Oscars' from the U.S. Academy of Motion Picture Arts?

7. Which film actress has won 3 'Oscars' in starring rôles?

8. Who wrote the song which had sold over 100 million recordings by 1970?

9. Who played in 85 consecutive Test cricket matches between 1955 and 1972?

10. What Parliamentary records are held by: (a) Dame Irene Ward; (b) Arthur Onslow?

11. What strange feat was performed by Charles Blondin, a rope-walker, on 4th July 1859?

12. Why was Prince Scipione Borghese so glad to reach Paris on 10th August 1907?

Record Breakers

1. The painting (*Portrait of Juan de Pareja*) sold at auction in 1970 for £2,310,000.

2. John Creasey.

3. In the House of Commons. He spoke for six hours on the subject of law reform.

4. Judge George Jeffreys, after the Duke of Monmouth's rebellion.

5. He is the only person to have won two prizes outright, for chemistry in 1954 and peace in 1962.

6. Walt Disney – 35.

7. Katherine Hepburn.

8. Irving Berlin – *White Christmas.*

9. Garfield Sobers, for the West Indies.

10. (*a*) the longest-serving woman Member of Parliament – 1931–45 and 1950–74; (*b*) the longest-serving Speaker – 1728–61.

11. He crossed Niagara Falls blindfold, on a tight-rope, with a wheelbarrow!

12. By doing so he had won the Peking–Paris motor-car race, a journey of 10,000 miles achieved in 61 days.

Religious Leaders

1. Who led the Children of Israel out of Egypt?

2. Which famous missionary came to England in 597 A.D. to try to convert the Anglo-Saxons to Christianity, and became the first Archbishop of Canterbury?

3. Who founded: (*a*) the Salvation Army; (*b*) the Mormons; (*c*) the Quakers (the Society of Friends); (*d*) the Jesuits (the Society of Jesus)?

4. Who was Zoroaster (or Zarathustra)?

5. Who founded the Methodist Church?

6. Can you say approximately when the following were alive: (*a*) Buddha; (*b*) Mahomet?

7. Who were: (*a*) John Wycliffe; (*b*) Savonarola?

8. What was the special claim to fame of Nicholas Breakspear of Hertfordshire?

9. Who were: (*a*) John Knox; (*b*) the Venerable Bede?

10. Name the sixteenth-century French theologian and Protestant reformer who gave his name to a religious doctrine.

11. Name the Dutch scholar and humanist who in the early sixteenth century attacked the abuses of the church and was pre-eminent in the Revival of Learning.

12. Name the German religious reformer of the early sixteenth century who was the founder of the Protestant Reformation.

Religious Leaders

1. Moses.

2. St. Augustine.

3. (a) General William Booth in 1865; (b) Joseph Smith in 1830; (c) George Fox in about 1650; (d) Ignatius Loyola in 1540.

4. A Persian prophet of the sixth century B.C. who founded the religion known as Zoroastrianism.

5. John Wesley (1703–91) in 1738.

6. (a) c. 552–472 B.C.;   (b) c. A.D. 570–632.

7. (a) a church reformer (c. 1320–84) who attacked the established practices of the church, and introduced a famous translation of the Bible; (b) an Italian religious reformer (1452–98) who attacked the Medici tyranny and became leader of Florence.

8. He was the only Englishman ever to become Pope, as Adrian IV (1154–9).

9. (a) a theologian and preacher (c 1505–72) who was the leader of the Scottish Reformation; (b) a Benedictine monk, writer, teacher, historian and theologian (c. 673–735) who was pre-eminent in Anglo-Saxon literature.

10. John Calvin (1509–64).

11. Desiderius Erasmus (1466–1536).

12. Martin Luther (1483–1546).

Sailors

1. (a) What was Nelson's naval rank at Trafalgar? (b) How old was he when he first went to sea? (c) In which battle did he first distinguish himself?

2. Which great English admiral did not become a sailor until he was fifty years old?

3. Who was officially in command of the Navy at the time of the defeat of the Spanish Armada?

4. Who were John and Sebastian Cabot?

5. What was similar about the deaths of Magellan and Captain Cook?

6. Who was Sir Henry Morgan?

7. Who were: (a) Sir John Franklin (1786–1847); (b) Sir Martin Frobisher (c. 1539–94); (c) Matthew Flinders (1774–1814)?

8. Name the English sailor who went round the world 1740–44 and later re-organized the Navy.

9. What happened to Admiral John Byng at Portsmouth in 1757?

10. What happened to Captain Bligh after the mutiny on the *Bounty*? Where did the mutineers settle?

11. Who commanded the British fleet at; (a) the battle of Jutland, 1916; (b) the battle of the Nile, 1798?

12. The First Sea Lord from 1943 to 1946, and the First Sea Lord from 1946 to 1948 had the same surname. What was it?

Sailors

1. (*a*) Vice-Admiral;   (*b*) 12;
   (*c*) St. Vincent, 1797.

2. Robert Blake (1599–1657).

3. Lord Howard of Effingham was Lord High Admiral.

4. Italian-born father and son who settled in Bristol and explored the coasts of North America in the fifteenth and sixteenth centuries.

5. They were both killed by natives, Magellan in the Philippines and Cook in Hawaii.

6. A Welsh buccaneer who was knighted by Charles II, and became deputy-governor of Jamaica.

7. (*a*) English explorer who disappeared on an Arctic expedition in search of the north-west passage; (*b*) English navigator who attempted to find the north-west passage across the Arctic; (*c*) English sailor who explored the coasts of Australia.

8. Admiral Lord Anson (1697–1762).

9. He was shot for neglect of duty in leaving the island of Minorca to its fate.

10. Bligh arrived at Timor, near Java, after an incredible journey of 3,600 miles in a small boat. The mutineers settled on Pitcairn Island.

11. (*a*) Admiral Sir John Jellicoe; (*b*) Admiral Nelson.

12. Cunningham.

Saints

1. What connection has St. Catherine of Alexandria with the firework named 'Catherine Wheel'?

2. Name the patron saints of England, Scotland, Wales and Ireland.

3. Which of the above were real persons and when did they live?

4. Name the patron saint of: (a) children; (b) shoemakers; (c) travellers; (d) housewives.

5. Who are the Latter-Day Saints?

6. Who was canonized nearly 500 years after her death?

7. Which English king was canonized in 1161, nearly 100 years after his death?

8. Of which saints are these the emblems: (a) a winged lion; (b) a horse and dragon; (c) three golden balls?

9. Which famous English statesman was canonized exactly 400 years after his death in 1535?

10. Which legendary saint was described as a giant who carried the child Jesus across a river?

11. Only one of the following saints was *not* a real person. Which one? Columba, Oswald, Michael, Gregory, Hilda, Wilfrid, Clement, Wenceslas, Swithun.

12. Name the saint who founded the Grey Friars and is famous for his kindness to animals.

Saints

1. According to legend she was a fourth-century martyr who was sentenced by the Roman emperor Maximinus to death by means of a spiked wheel. She was adopted as the patron saint of wheelwrights.

2. St. George, St. Andrew, St. David and St. Patrick.

3. All were real except St. George. St. David lived in the sixth century A.D. and founded a monastery in Pembrokeshire, St. Patrick was a Romano-Briton of the early fifth century A.D. and St. Andrew was one of the 12 apostles.

4. (a) St. Nicholas;   (b) St. Crispin;
   (c) St. Christopher;   (d) St. Anne.

5. The Mormons.

6. St. Joan of Arc (died 1431, canonized 1920).

7. Edward the Confessor.

8. (a) St. Mark;   (b) St. George;
   (c) St. Nicholas.

9. St. Thomas More (1478–1535).

10. St. Christopher.

11. St. Michael.

12. St. Francis of Assisi (c. 1181–1226).

Scientists

1. Name the famous scientist and Presbyterian minister who emigrated to America because his theological opinions were unpopular in England.

2. Who first discovered these elements: (*a*) oxygen; (*b*) radium; (*c*) hydrogen?

3. What great discoveries were made by a former London bookbinder's apprentice in the nineteenth century?

4. For what were these men famous: (*a*) Lavoisier; (*b*) Torricelli; (*c*) Bunsen; (*d*) Plimsoll?

5. Name the millionaire son of a duke who was a famous chemist and discovered the constituents of water.

6. Name four of the seven units of electrical measurement named after their originators.

7. What researches or inventions were the following men connected with: (*a*) Bessemer; (*b*) Rutherford; (*c*) Crookes; (*d*) Fox-Talbot?

8. Could (*a*) Faraday have switched on an electric light in his home; (*b*) George III have seen gas lighting in the street; (*c*) Byron have taken a ride in a steam locomotive?

9. Archimedes supposedly discovered his famous 'Principle' while taking a bath. Can you state briefly what it is?

10. What are: (*a*) Mendeléeff's 'Table'; (*b*) Daltonism?

11. Who discovered or isolated six different elements in the years 1807–08?

12. What important discoveries did these men make: (*a*) Edward Jenner; (*b*) Alexander Fleming; (*c*) Robert Koch; (*d*) Ronald Ross?

Scientists

1. Joseph Priestley (1733–1804).

2. (a) K. W. Scheele, about 1772; (b) Pierre and Marie Curie, 1898; (c) Henry Cavendish, 1766.

3. Michael Faraday (1791–1867) made important discoveries in electricity and electromagnetism, including the induction of electric currents and the identity of electrification.

4. (a) French chemist who evolved the modern theory of combustion; (b) inventor of the barometer; (c) inventor of the Bunsen burner and discoverer of the element caesium; (d) originator of the Plimsoll line on ships.

5. Henry Cavendish (1731–1810).

6. Farad (Faraday); Volt (Volta); Joule; Henry; Ampère; Ohm; Coulomb.

7. (a) invented the process of converting cast iron into steel; (b) nuclear physics; (c) invented the radiometer and sun-glasses; (d) early photographic experiments.

8. (a) No. He died in 1867 and light bulbs were invented in 1880; (b) Yes. Gas lighting was seen in the Strand in 1803; (c) Yes. Trevithick drove his locomotive in London in 1803.

9. The apparent loss of weight of a body immersed in a liquid is equal to the weight of the liquid displaced.

10. (a) list of elements by atomic weight; (b) colour-blindness.

11. Humphry Davy (1778–1829).

12. (a) vaccination against smallpox; (b) penicillin; (c) tuberculosis germ; (d) malaria parasite.

Seventeenth-Century People

1. What was 'ship-money' and what happened when John Hampden refused to pay it?

2. Why was Thomas Wentworth, Earl of Strafford, executed in 1641?

3. Who were Robert Catesby, Thomas Winter, Thomas Percy and John Wright?

4. Whose perjuries caused the death of some 35 innocent Catholics in 1678–80?

5. What official position was held by Samuel Pepys?

6. The year 1642 witnessed the death of a great Italian astronomer and the birth of the greatest English mathematician. Who were they?

7. Who was Robert Boyle (1627–91)?

8. Can you name another famous English diarist of the seventeenth century, apart from Pepys?

9. In what field were these men famous: (a) Christiaan Huygens; (b) René Descartes; (c) Robert Herrick; (d) Henry Purcell?

10. Who were Jean Racine, Pierre Corneille and Jean-Baptiste Molière?

11. Name the great English wood-carver and sculptor born in 1648.

12. Why was John Bunyan imprisoned?

Seventeenth-Century People

1. It was a tax levied by Charles I without the consent of Parliament. Hampden was prosecuted by the Crown and eventually lost his case.

2. He was impeached for high treason on several charges, and under pressure Charles I signed his death warrant to appease Parliament.

3. They were the leaders, with Guy Fawkes, of the Gunpowder Plot (1605).

4. Titus Oates, who had invented a Jesuit plot to stir up public hostility to the Catholics.

5. Secretary to the Admiralty.

6. Galileo and Newton.

7. Famous chemist and physicist, formulator of Boyle's Law relating to gases.

8. John Evelyn (1620–1706).

9. (*a*) astronomy and physics; (*b*) philosophy and mathematics; (*c*) poetry; (*d*) music.

10. They were all French dramatists.

11. Grinling Gibbons.

12. For preaching and holding services not in accordance with the ritual of the church, i.e. in places other than a parish church.

Singers and Dancers

1. Who was known as 'The Swedish Nightingale'?

2. Name the Austrian-born tenor who became a naturalized British subject and died in Australia.

3. Where were the following singers born: (*a*) Enrico Caruso; (*b*) Nellie Melba; (*c*) Kathleen Ferrier; (*d*) Beniamino Gigli; (*e*) Joan Sutherland?

4. Name the four members of the 'Beatles' group.

5. Complete these 'pairs': (*a*) Anne Ziegler and ....; (*b*) Jeannette Macdonald and ....

6. Who was called the 'Sweetheart of the Forces'?

7. Who is the odd one out of these: Leonide Massine; Anna Pavlova; Nadia Nerina; Rudolf Nureyev?

8. Name the Irish-born ballerina and former member of Diaghilev's company who became Director of the Royal Ballet.

9. Who is the odd one out of these: Robert Helpmann; Anton Dolin; Dame Alicia Markova; Margot Fonteyn?

10. Which dancer: (*a*) partnered Ginger Rogers in several films; (*b*) was the star of the film *The Red Shoes*?

11. Name the Russian dancer born in 1888 who became insane in 1917 until his death in 1950.

12. Name the great Russian bass singer who came of a poor family and died in Paris in 1938.

Singers and Dancers

1. Jenny Lind (1820–87).

2. Richard Tauber (1891–1948).

3. (*a*) Italy;   (*b*) Australia;
   (*c*) England;   (*d*) Italy;
   (*e*) Australia.

4. George Harrison, Paul Macartney, John Lennon and Ringo Starr.

5. (*a*) Webster Booth;   (*b*) Nelson Eddy.

6. Vera Lynn.

7. Nadia Nerina was born in South Africa, the other three in Russia.

8. Dame Ninette de Valois.

9. Robert Helpmann was born in Australia, the others in Britain.

10. (*a*) Fred Astaire;   (*b*) Moira Shearer.

11. Vaslav Nijinsky.

12. Feodor Chaliapin.

Soldiers

1. Name the British general killed by the Mahdi at Khartoum in 1885. Who commanded the relief expedition which arrived too late to save him?

2. Name the four great commanders in history who never lost an important battle.

3. What were the names of: (a) Duke of Wellington; (b) Duke of Marlborough; (c) Duke of Albemarle?

4. Which British generals were killed at: (a) Corunna in 1809; (b) Quebec in 1759?

5. Name: (a) the British field-marshal drowned near the Orkneys in 1916; (b) the French marshal who became King of Sweden.

6. Who relieved whom at: (a) Mafeking; (b) Ladysmith?

7. On which side were these American Civil War generals: Lee, Grant, Sherman, Jackson?

8. Who were the victorious commanders at these battles: (a) El Alamein; (b) Naseby; (c) Bannockburn; (d) Blenheim?

9. The French general Foch first saw action in 1914. What was remarkable about that?

10. Which two famous commanders fought their last battles at the age of 32?

11. Who marched his armies, elephants included, over the Alps?

12. Name: (a) the Prussian field-marshal whose forces assisted Wellington at Waterloo; (b) the first British field-marshal to rise from the ranks.

Soldiers

1. Charles Gordon. Viscount Wolseley.

2. Julius Caesar, Alexander the Great, Oliver Cromwell and the Duke of Wellington.

3. (*a*) Arthur Wellesley;　　(*b*) John Churchill;
   (*c*) George Monk.

4. (*a*) Sir John Moore;　　(*b*) James Wolfe.

5. (*a*) Kitchener;　　(*b*) Bernadotte.

6. (*a*) Field-Marshal Lord Roberts relieved Colonel Baden-Powell; (*b*) General Sir Redvers Buller relieved General Sir George White.

7. Grant and Sherman were on the Federal side (the 'North'), Lee and Jackson on the Confederate side (the 'South').

8. (*a*) Montgomery;　　(*b*) Cromwell and Fairfax;
   (*c*) Robert I (the 'Bruce');　(*d*) Marlborough.

9. He was 62 at the time and had been a soldier for 44 years.

10. Alexander the Great and General James Wolfe.

11. Hannibal in 218 B.C.

12. (*a*) Blucher;　　(*b*) Sir William Robertson.

Sportsmen

1. Who has been men's singles tennis champion at Wimbledon the most times since 1945?

2. What have the following in common: Borotra, Cochet, Lacoste?

3. Which jockey was the first to win the Derby three years running?

4. Who was the first man to run a mile in less than four minutes?

5. With which sports are these associated: (*a*) Mike Hawthorn; (*b*) Joe Davis; (*c*) Gary Player; (*d*) Fred Archer; (*e*) Mick McManus; (*f*) Reg Harris?

6. Which heavyweight boxer was: (*a*) world champion for 11 years; (*b*) the oldest ever to be world champion; (*c*) the last British world champion?

7. Ken Rosewall was the losing finalist in four Wimbledon singles matches. Name two of his victorious opponents.

8. Which English international full-back and Test cricketer also held the world long-jump record?

9. Can you name the oldest and youngest racing drivers ever to be world champion?

10. Which jockey won the Derby six times between 1954 and 1972?

11. What have the following in common: Max Faulkner, Fred Daly, Henry Cotton, Tony Jacklin?

12. What was Dr. Emannuel Lasker's record?

Sportsmen

1. Rod Laver – four times.

2. All French tennis champions of the nineteen-twenties.

3. Steve Donoghue, 1921–3.

4. Roger Bannister in 1954.

5. (a) motor-racing;   (b) billiards and snooker;
   (c) golf;   (d) horse-racing;
   (e) wrestling;   (f) cycling.

6. (a) Joe Louis, 1937–48; (b) Jersey Joe Walcott, 37 in 1951; (c) Bob Fitzsimmons, 1897–9.

7. Drobny (1954), Hoad (1956), Newcombe (1970) and Connors (1974).

8. C. B. Fry.

9. Juan Manuel Fangio, 46 in 1957, and Emerson Fittipaldi, 25 in 1972.

10. Lester Piggott.

11. All British winners of the British Open Golf Championship since 1947.

12. He was world chess champion from 1894 to 1921.

Sportswomen

1. Which French tennis star won the ladies' singles final at Wimbledon five times in succession?

2. What lawn tennis record is held by Maureen Connolly and Margaret Court?

3. What was achieved by Diane Leather in 1957?

4. Who is the odd one out of these: Christine Truman, Ann Haydon, Angela Mortimer, Dorothy Round?

5. Who or what was Flanagan?

6. Who was Miss Joyce Wethered (Lady Heathcoat-Amory)?

7. Which American lady golf champion also won Olympic gold medals for the javelin and hurdles?

8. With which sports do you associate: (a) Sonja Henie; (b) Althea Gibson; (c) Fanny Blankers-Koen?

9. What record is held by horse-rider Pat Smythe?

10. What did Helen Wills (Mrs. F. S. Moody) win eight times between 1927 and 1938?

11. What did Gertrude Ederle achieve in 1926 that Florence Chadwick achieved 25 years later in the opposite direction?

12. Who won the Pentathlon at the 1972 Olympic Games?

Sportswomen

1. Suzanne Lenglen.

2. They won all four major singles championships in one year.

3. She was the first woman to run a mile in less than five minutes.

4. Christine Truman. All the others have been Wimbledon singles champions.

5. The famous horse ridden by show-jumper Pat Smythe.

6. Probably the greatest lady golfer of all time. She was British champion in 1922, 1924, 1925 and 1929.

7. 'Babe' Zaharias.

8. (*a*) ice-skating;   (*b*) tennis; (*c*) athletics.

9. She won the Ladies' Show-jumping Championship eight times.

10. The Wimbledon ladies' singles championship.

11. She swam the English Channel from France to England.

12. Mary Peters.

Television Personalities

1. Who was the first Director-General of the B.B.C.?

2. Who played the part of: (a) 'The Baron'; (b) Callan;
   (c) 'Danger Man'; (d) 'The Saint'?

3. Who are: (a) the two 'Ronnies'; (b) Steptoe and son?

4. What have these in common: Kenneth Kendall,
   Gordon Honeycombe, Richard Baker?

5. Who played the part of: (a) Hudson the butler in
   Upstairs, Downstairs; (b) Captain Mainwaring in *Dad's
   Army*; (c) Frank Spencer in *Some mothers do 'ave 'em*?

6. Who was the B.B.C.'s first war correspondent in 1939?

7. With which sports do you associate:
   (a) Max Robertson;   (b) Harry Carpenter;
   (c) E. W. ('Jim') Swanton;   (d) Jimmy Hill?

8. Who played these parts: (a) Marker (in *Private Eye*);
   (b) Barlow; (d) Ironside; (e) Maigret?

9. (a) Who was the antiques expert on *Going for a Song*?
   (b) Who looks at *The Sky at Night*?

10. Who was the first resident compere of: (a) *University
    Challenge*; (b) *The Generation Game*; (c) *Sale of the
    Century*; (d) *Call My Bluff*?

11. Who introduced the series: (a) *Civilization*; (b) *The
    Ascent of Man*?

12. Who played the part of: (a) Lord Peter Wimsey; (b)
    Father Brown?

Television Personalities

1. Lord Reith.

2. (*a*) Steve Forrest;   (*b*) Edward Woodward;
   (*c*) Patrick McGoohan;   (*d*) Roger Moore.

3. (*a*) Ronnie Barker and Ronnie Corbett; (*b*) Wilfred
   Brambell and Harry H. Corbett.

4. All news-readers.

5. (*a*) Gordon Jackson;   (*b*) Arthur Lowe;
   (*c*) Michael Crawford.

6. Richard Dimbleby.

7. (*a*) tennis;   (*b*) boxing;
   (*c*) cricket;   (*d*) football.

8. (*a*) Alfred Burke;   (*b*) Stratford Johns;
   (*c*) William Conrad;   (*d*) Raymond Burr;
   (*e*) Rupert Davies.

9. (*a*) Arthur Negus;   (*b*) Patrick Moore.

10. (*a*) Bamber Gascoigne;   (*b*) Bruce Forsyth;
    (*c*) Nicholas Parsons;   (*d*) Robert Robinson.

11. (*a*) Sir Kenneth, now Lord Clark; (*b*) Dr. Jacob
    Bronowski.

12. (*a*) Ian Carmichael;   (*b*) Kenneth More.

Things Named After People

1. Can you name a road-making material named after its inventor?

2. What is shrapnel, and why is it so-called?

3. Which two noble soldiers of Crimean war fame gave their names to: (a) a woollen waistcoat; (b) a type of overcoat?

4. Who gave their names to the two great Roman walls constructed in the north of Britain?

5. Which well-known flower is named after a sixteenth-century German professor of medicine?

6. Why were 'bloomers' so-called?

7. Why is a sandwich called by that name?

8. Who gave their names to: (a) a kind of large sofa; (b) a light travelling-bag; (c) a type of rubber boot; (d) a kind of short overcoat?

9. Who gave his name to a stately burial-place or tomb?

10. Why are policemen sometimes called 'bobbies'?

11. Name two types of carriage named after people.

12. Which one of these is not named after a person: dahlia, forsythia, gardenia, lupin, loganberry, greengage?

Things Named After People

1. Tarmac. (J. L. Macadam).

2. A hollow shell containing bullets which bursts by means of a time fuse, invented by Major H. Shrapnel in 1784.

3. (*a*) Cardigan;   (*b*) Raglan.

4. Hadrian (Hadrian's Wall) and Antoninus Pius (Antonine Wall).

5. Fuchsia (Leonhard Fuchs).

6. Amelia Bloomer (1818–94) popularized them as part of the campaign for women's rights.

7. It was named after the fourth Earl of Sandwich who, reluctant to leave the gaming-table, ordered some slices of bread, and meat to put between them.

8. (*a*) an Earl of Chesterfield; (*b*) W. E. Gladstone; (*c*) the Duke of Wellington; (*d*) the second Earl Spencer.

9. Mausolus, ancient King of Caria – (mausoleum).

10. After Sir Robert Peel.

11. Brougham; hansom; stanhope.

12. Lupin.

Travellers

1. Which parts of the world were explored by: (*a*) Marco Polo; (*b*) Mungo Park; (*c*) Edward Eyre?

2. Who wrote these books of travel: (*a*) *Eothen*; (*b*) *The Path to Rome*; (*c*) *The Worst Journey in the World*?

3. What have these people in common: John Leland, Daniel Defoe, William Cobbett, Celia Fiennes?

4. (*a*) Who was the first man to sail alone around the world? (*b*) Who was the first man to sail non-stop alone around the world?

5. Who first climbed: (*a*) the Matterhorn; (*b*) Mt. Everest?

6. Where did Charles Darwin go between 1831 and 1836?

7. Name the German naturalist who explored South America 1799–1804 and Central Asia in 1829.

8. Who journeyed to the Hebrides together in 1773 and later wrote accounts of their travels?

9. What happened to R. O. Burke and W. J. Wills in 1861?

10. Who wrote: (*a*) *The Ascent of Everest*; (*b*) *Pilgrimage to Al-Medinah and Meccah*?

11. Who travelled overland to the South Pole in 1957–8?

12. Who sailed around the world in: (*a*) *Gipsy Moth IV*; (*b*) *Lively Lady*?

Travellers

1. (a) India and China;   (b) Africa;
 (c) Australia.

2. (a) A. W. Kinglake;   (b) Hilaire Belloc;
 (c) A. Cherry-Garrard.

3. They all travelled through England at various times and wrote books about their travels.

4. (a) Captain Joshua Slocum, 1895–8; (b) Robin Knox-Johnston, 1968–9.

5. (a) Edward Whymper in 1865; (b) Edmund Hillary and Sherpa Tenzing in 1953.

6. He sailed on board H.M.S. *Beagle* on its scientific exploration of the Atlantic, Pacific and South America.

7. Baron Friedrich von Humboldt (1769–1859).

8. Samuel Johnson and James Boswell.

9. They died of starvation on the return journey after crossing the continent of Australia.

10. (a) John Hunt;   (b) Sir Richard Burton.

11. Vivian Fuchs and Edmund Hillary, on the British Commonwealth Trans-Antarctic Expedition.

12. (a) Francis Chichester;   (b) Alec Rose.

Twentieth-Century People

1. Name: (*a*) the Austrian Chancellor murdered in 1934; (*b*) the Czechoslovakian Foreign Minister who died after falling from a high window in 1948.

2. Who are or were: 'Duke' Ellington, 'Count' Basie and Nat 'King' Cole?

3. Which woman became Prime Minister of: (*a*) Israel in 1969; (*b*) India in 1966?

4. Which former Labour Minister was imprisoned as a Fascist in 1940?

5. Who are associated with these places: (*a*) Lambarené; (*b*) El Alamein; (*c*) Beaulieu Abbey; (*d*) Ayot St. Lawrence?

6. Who was Chancellor of the Exchequer in the first British Labour government?

7. The Treaty of Versailles in 1919 was virtually dictated by which three men?

8. Who was born on: (*a*) 21st April 1926; (*b*) 10th June 1921?

9. Can you name three British Chancellors of the Exchequer since 1964?

10. Name four of the first ten people in the Order of Precedence in England.

11. Can you name two of the seven Popes of this century?

12. Who were: (*a*) Joseph McCarthy; (*b*) Kwame Nkrumah; (*c*) Heinrich Himmler; (*d*) Osbert Sitwell?

Twentieth-Century People

1. (*a*) Engelbert Dollfuss; (*b*) Jan Masaryk.

2. The first two – composer, bandleader and pianist; Nat 'King' Cole – singer.

3. (*a*) Golda Meir; (*b*) Indira Gandhi.

4. Sir Oswald Mosley.

5. (*a*) Albert Schweitzer; (*b*) Viscount Montgomery;
   (*c*) Lord Montagu; (*d*) George Bernard Shaw.

6. Philip Snowden.

7. Woodrow Wilson, Lloyd George and Clemenceau.

8. (*a*) Queen Elizabeth II; (*b*) Prince Philip, Duke of Edinburgh.

9. Maudling, Callaghan, Jenkins, MacLeod, Barber, Healey.

10. The Queen, the Duke of Edinburgh, the Prince of Wales, Prince Andrew, Prince Edward, the Duke of Gloucester, the Archbishop of Canterbury, the Lord High Chancellor, the Archbishop of York and the Prime Minister.

11. Leo XIII, Pius X, Benedict XV, Pius XI, Pius XII John XXIII and Paul VI.

12. (*a*) American senator who held anti-Communist 'witch-hunts'; (*b*) first President of Ghana; (*c*) chief of the Gestapo, the Nazi secret police; (*d*) English author and poet.

Untimely Ends and Sudden Deaths

1. Which one of these was *not* beheaded: Thomas More, Thomas Cromwell, Cardinal Wolsey, Walter Raleigh?

2. Which English poet: (*a*) was drowned while sailing in Italy; (*b*) died of rheumatic fever in Greece; (*c*) was killed in a tavern fight in Deptford?

3. Who was killed in a flying-boat crash in Scotland in 1942?

4. Who was assassinated by: (*a*) Charlotte Corday; (*b*) John Wilkes Booth; (*c*) Gavrilo Princip?

5. Which famous French scientist was executed on the guillotine in 1794?

6. How did the following meet their deaths: (*a*) Socrates; (*b*) St. Paul; (*c*) Joan of Arc; (*d*) Clive of India?

7. Who was murdered in Canterbury cathedral in 1170?

8. Name the American negro leader assassinated in 1968.

9. Who was assassinated by: (*a*) a Hindu fanatic on 30th January 1948; (*b*) an ex-naval officer at Portsmouth in 1628; (*c*) a half-crazy bankrupt in 1812?

10. At what age did the following die (say to within 3 years): (*a*) John Keats; (*b*) P. B. Shelley; (*c*) Alexander the Great; (*d*) Edward VI; (*e*) Grace Darling; (*f*) Franz Schubert?

11. How did Lady Jane Grey, Mary Queen of Scots and Anne Boleyn meet their deaths?

12. Which is the odd one out of these: Harry Hawker, Hon. C. S. Rolls, Charles Lindbergh, Sir John Alcock?

Untimely Ends and Sudden Deaths

1. Cardinal Wolsey.

2. (a) Shelley (1822);   (b) Byron (1824);
   (c) Marlowe (1593).

3. George, Duke of Kent.

4. (a) Jean Paul Marat; (b) Abraham Lincoln; (c) Archduke Ferdinand of Austria, at Sarajevo, 1914.

5. Lavoisier.

6. (a) condemned to death by drinking poison; (b) executed in Rome; (c) burnt at the stake in Rouen market-place; (d) committed suicide by cutting his throat.

7. Thomas Becket, Archbishop of Canterbury.

8. Martin Luther King.

9. (a) Mahatma Gandhi; (b) George Villiers, Duke of Buckingham; (c) Spencer Perceval, British Prime Minister.

10. (a) 25;   (b) 29;
    (c) 32;   (d) 15;
    (e) 26;   (f) 31.

11. They were all beheaded.

12. Charles Lindbergh. The others were all killed in aeroplane accidents.

Was It Possible?

1. (*a*) Could Michael Faraday have used the telephone? (*b*) Could the Duke of Wellington have been photographed?

2. (*a*) Could Queen Elizabeth I have worn spectacles? (*b*) Could King George IV have met the future Queen Victoria?

3. (*a*) Could George Washington have used blotting-paper? (*b*) Could James Boswell have seen gas lighting?

4. (*a*) Could Mrs. Abraham Lincoln have used a sewing machine? (*b*) Could Charles Dickens have listened to a phonograph?

5. (*a*) Could Gladstone have been X-rayed? (*b*) Could Queen Victoria have taken aspirin?

6. (*a*) Could Nelson have worn a macintosh? (*b*) Could Disraeli have used a safety-razor?

7. (*a*) Could Sir Henry Stanley have gone to the cinema? (*b*) Could Florence Nightingale have seen an aeroplane?

8. (*a*) Could Tennyson have taken a ride in a motor-car? (*b*) Could he have used a typewriter?

9. (*a*) Could Brunel have smoked a cigarette? (*b*) Could Prince Albert have pulled a Christmas cracker?

10. Which of these could have travelled by steam passenger railway: Wordsworth, Constable, Cobbett, George III?

11. Which of these could have used adhesive postage stamps: Jane Austen, the Brontë sisters, Coleridge, G. Stephenson?

12. Which of these could have seen a public television broadcast: G. K. Chesterton, Baden-Powell, Asquith, James Barrie?

Was It Possible?

1. (*a*) No. He died in 1867 and the telephone came in 1876. (*b*) Yes. The first photograph was taken in 1826.

2. (*a*) Yes. Spectacles were in use in the fourteenth century. (*b*) Yes. He died in 1830 and she was born in 1819.

3. (*a*) Yes, but very unlikely as it was not in general use. (*b*) No. He died in 1795 and gas lighting came in 1801.

4. (*a*) Yes. The first domestic machine was made in 1851. (*b*) No. He died in 1870 and the phonograph appeared in 1877.

5. (*a*) Yes. He died in 1898 and X-rays were discovered in 1895. (*b*) No. It was introduced to Britain in 1905.

6. (*a*) No. The macintosh was introduced in 1823. (*b*) No. The safety-razor was invented in 1901.

7. (*a*) Yes. He died in 1904; the first cinema opened in 1901. (*b*) Yes. She died in 1910; the first flight in England was in 1908.

8. (*a*) No. He died in 1892; the first car in Britain was in 1894. (*b*) Yes. The typewriter came to Britain in 1889.

9. (*a*) Yes. He died in 1859; the first cigarette was in 1851. (*b*) Yes. Crackers were introduced in the eighteen-forties.

10. All except George III.

11. The Brontë sisters and George Stephenson.

12. All except Asquith, who died a few months before the first broadcast in 1928.

When Did They Live?

1. In which century did the following live: (a) Alfred the Great; (b) Mozart; (c) Attila the Hun?

2. Which one of these was not alive in 1480: Copernicus, Caxton, Columbus, Raleigh, Thomas More?

3. Which one of these could not have seen the Great Fire of London: Pepys, Defoe, Wren, Swift, Charles II?

4. Were the following alive at the same time: (a) Richard Cromwell and John Wesley; (b) Marlborough and Charles I?

5. Who is the odd one out of these: Robert the Bruce, Chaucer, Dante, Edward I, Marco Polo?

6. In which century did the following live: (a) Richard II; (b) Nero; (c) Francis Drake?

7. Which one of these was not alive in 1945: Lloyd-George, Franklin Roosevelt, H. G. Wells, Sir Henry Wood?

8. Which one of these was alive in 1900: R. L. Stevenson, John Ruskin, Louis Pasteur, W. E. Gladstone?

9. Were the following alive at the same time: (a) Tennyson and George VI; (b) James Watt and Dickens?

10. What was remarkable about the span of life of Isaac Newton (1642–1727)?

11. What have the following in common: Edmund Blunden, Rupert Brooke, Robert Graves, Siegfried Sassoon?

12. Who is the odd one out: Captain Cook, John Milton, Marie Antoinette?

When Did They Live?

1. (*a*) *c*. 849–99;   (*b*) 1756–91;
   (*c*) *c*. 406–53.

2. Sir Walter Raleigh (1552–1618).

3. Swift.

4. (*a*) Yes. Richard Cromwell died in 1712 and John Wesley was born in 1703; (*b*) No. John Churchill, Duke of Marlborough, was born in 1650 and Charles I died in 1649.

5. Chaucer (1340–1400). All the others were born in the thirteenth century and died in the early fourteenth century.

6. (*a*) 1367–1400;   (*b*) A.D. 37–68;
   (*c*) 1541–96.

7. Sir Henry Wood died in 1944.

8. John Ruskin died in that year.

9. (*a*) No. Tennyson died in 1892 and George VI was born in 1895; (*b*) Yes. James Watt died in 1819 and Dickens was born in 1812.

10. He lived during the reigns of eight sovereigns or rulers, from Charles I to George I (in fact almost into the reign of George II).

11. They were all in action on the Western Front in the first World War. Rupert Brooke was killed there.

12. John Milton lived in the seventeenth century, the other two in the eighteenth.

Who Said That?

1. Who said that England was 'a nation of shopkeepers'?

2. Who said: (*a*) 'We are not amused.' (*b*) 'My patience is exhausted.'

3. 'I awoke one morning and found myself famous.' Who said that, and on what occasion?

4. Who wrote: 'He who can, does. He who cannot, teaches.'?

5. Who wrote: (*a*) 'They also serve who only stand and wait.' (*b*) 'Man is born free, and everywhere he is in chains.'?

6. Which Prime Minister said: 'What is our task? To make Britain a fit country for heroes to live in.'?

7. Which Prime Minister, referring to Africa, said: 'The wind of change is blowing through the continent.'?

8. What was said about 'Patriotism' by: (*a*) Dr. Johnson; (*b*) Edith Cavell?

9. Who wrote: (*a*) 'To err is human, to forgive, divine.' (*b*) 'For fools rush in where angels fear to tread.' (*c*) 'Hope springs eternal in the human breast.'?

10. Complete these quotations: (*a*) 'Let us therefore brace ourselves to our duties . . .' (Churchill); (*b*) 'That this nation, under God, shall have . . .' (Lincoln); (*c*) 'If you can keep your head . . .' (Kipling).

11. Who said: 'I look upon all the world as my parish.'?

12. Who wrote: (*a*) 'No man but a blockhead ever wrote except for money.' (*b*) 'The Moving Finger writes: and, having writ, Moves on.'?

Who Said That?

1. Napoleon Bonaparte.

2. (a) Queen Victoria;   (b) Adolf Hitler.

3. Lord Byron, on the publication of *Childe Harold*.

4. George Bernard Shaw.

5. (a) John Milton;   (b) Jean-Jacques Rousseau.

6. Lloyd George.

7. Harold Macmillan.

8. (a) 'Patriotism is the last refuge of a scoundrel.' (b) 'Patriotism is not enough.'

9. All were written by Alexander Pope.

10. (a) '. . . and so bear ourselves that, if the British Empire and its Commonwealth last for a thousand years, men will still say, "This was their finest hour".'
    (b) '. . . a new birth of freedom, and that government of the people, by the people, for the people, shall not perish from the earth.'
    (c) '. . . when all about you
    Are losing theirs and blaming it on you.'

11. John Wesley.

12. (a) Dr. Johnson;   (b) Omar Khayyam.

Who Was the First?

1. (*a*) Who was the first man to orbit the earth in space?
   (*b*) Who were the first two men to set foot on the Moon?

2. Who was the first man to swim the English Channel?

3. Who was the first Secretary-General of the United Nations, and who succeeded him?

4. What was achieved by Marconi in December 1901?

5. Who was the first man to: (*a*) print a book in England; (*b*) publish a book with photographic illustrations?

6. Who was the first 'disc jockey'?

7. What was invented by David Bushnell in 1776 and first used in the American War of Independence?

8. What distinction was gained by Lieutenant Charles Lucas, a naval officer, on 21st June 1854?

9. Who performed the world's first human heart transplant operation?

10. Which father and son were the first men to exceed 300 m.p.h. on land and water respectively?

11. What was introduced in 1680 by William Dockwra, and in 1840 by Rowland Hill?

12. Can you give the name of the first British Nobel prizewinner for *any* of these: literature; peace; chemistry; physics; medicine?

Who Was the First?

1. (*a*) Major Yuri Gagarin of Russia in 1961; (*b*) Neil Armstrong and Edwin Aldrin on 21st July 1969.

2. Matthew Webb in 1875.

3. Trygve Lie of Norway was succeeded by Dag Hammarskjold of Sweden.

4. He became the first man to transmit a wireless message across the Atlantic.

5. (*a*) William Caxton in 1477 (*The Dictes or Sayengis of the Philosophres*); (*b*) William Henry Fox Talbot in 1844 (*The Pencil of Nature*).

6. Christopher Stone in 1927.

7. The submarine.

8. He was the first man to be awarded the Victoria Cross.

9. Professor Christian Barnard of South Africa in 1967.

10. Sir Malcolm Campbell on land in 1935, and his son Donald Campbell on water in 1967.

11. The London Penny Post by Dockwra, and the adhesive postage stamp by Hill.

12. Literature – Rudyard Kipling, 1907; Peace – Sir William Cremer, 1903; Chemistry – Sir William Ramsay, 1904; Physics – Lord Rayleigh, 1904; Medicine – Sir Ronald Ross, 1902.

Writers

1. What have the following in common: Adolf Hitler, Daniel Defoe, John Bunyan, Walter Raleigh?

2. Which British author had the Swastika on the covers of the books he had written?

3. What have the following in common: (*a*) Conan Doyle, Somerset Maugham, A. J. Cronin; (*b*) Gibbon, Macaulay, Belloc, A. E. W. Mason?

4. Name four of the eight English and Irish winners of the Nobel prize for literature.

5. Which writers lived in these houses: (*a*) Max Gate; (*b*) Fonthill Abbey; (*c*) Gads Hill?

6. Which famous novelist: (*a*) fought in the Crimean War; (*b*) inaugurated the International Code of Signals for merchant shipping?

7. How long did Samuel Pepys live after the last entry in his diary?

8. (*a*) Whose body was buried in Westminster Abbey but his heart in Dorset? (*b*) Whose body was buried in Italy but his heart in Westminster Abbey?

9. Who wrote about these fictitious countries: (*a*) Shangri-La; (*b*) Utopia; (*c*) Erewhon; (*d*) Lilliput?

10. What other professions were followed by these writers: (*a*) Matthew Arnold; (*b*) Anthony Trollope; (*c*) Lewis Carroll?

11. Which two great writers both died on 23rd April 1616?

12. Who wrote: (*a*) *Rural Rides*; (*b*) *The Origin of Species* ...; (*c*) *Lavengro*; (*d*) *The Story of San Michele*?

Writers

1. They all wrote a famous book while in prison.

2. Rudyard Kipling.

3. (*a*) they were all doctors; (*b*) they were all Members of Parliament.

4. Rudyard Kipling, W. B. Yeats, G. B. Shaw, John Galsworthy, T. S. Eliot, Bertrand Russell, Winston Churchill, Samuel Beckett.

5. (*a*) Thomas Hardy;   (*b*) William Beckford; (*c*) Charles Dickens.

6. (*a*) Count Tolstoy;   (*b*) Captain Marryat.

7. 34 years, from 1669 to 1703.

8. (*a*) Thomas Hardy;   (*b*) P. B. Shelley.

9. (*a*) James Hilton;   (*b*) Thomas More; (*c*) Samuel Butler;   (*d*) Jonathan Swift.

10. (*a*) Inspector of Schools; (*b*) Post Office Inspector; (*c*) Mathematics lecturer at Oxford.

11. William Shakespeare and Miguel de Cervantes.

12. (*a*) William Cobbett;   (*b*) Charles Darwin; (*c*) George Borrow;   (*d*) Axel Munthe.

More Cricketers and Footballers

1. Name three cricketers and two footballers who have been knighted for their services to sport.

2. What have the following in common: R. E. Foster, A. Ducat, W. Watson, J. Arnold, H. Makepeace, C. A. Milton?

3. Who holds the record for the highest Test innings, and who made the second highest?

4. For which counties did these cricketers play: (a) T. E. Bailey; (b) C. Washbrook; (c) E. R. Dexter; (d) H. Larwood; (e) H. Verity; (f) R. E. Marshall?

5. Who captained Gloucestershire for 28 years, and who captained Yorkshire for 28 years?

6. What unique feat was achieved by Arthur Fagg in 1938 when playing for Kent against Essex?

7. Who captained the M.C.C. team on the famous 'body-line' tour of Australia in 1932–3?

8. Which of these was the manager of the F.A. Cup winners in 1974: Don Revie, Bill Shankly, Brian Clough, Alf Ramsey?

9. Who is the odd one out of these: Frank Swift, Sam Bartram, Neil Franklin, Gil Merrick, Ted Ditchburn?

10. How old was Billy Meredith when he played for Wales against England in 1920: 25: 30: 35: 40: 45: 50?

11. Has a German-born player ever appeared in a Wembley Cup Final?

12. Who was the captain of the England team that won the World Cup in 1966?

More Cricketers and Footballers

1. Cricketers – Donald Bradman, Leonard Hutton, Frank Worrell, Pelham Warner, Jack Hobbs, Garfield Sobers. Footballers – Stanley Matthews, Alf Ramsey, Matt Busby, Stanley Rous.

2. All played for England both at cricket and Association football.

3. Garfield Sobers – 365 not out for West Indies v. Pakistan in 1958. Len Hutton 364 for England v. Australia in 1938.

4. (*a*) Essex;   (*b*) Lancashire;
   (*c*) Sussex;   (*d*) Notts;
   (*e*) Yorkshire;   (*f*) Hampshire.

5. W. G. Grace (1871–98) and Lord Hawke (1883–1910).

6. He scored a double-century in each innings.

7. D. R. Jardine.

8. Bill Shankly – Liverpool.

9. Neil Franklin was a centre-half, all the others were goal-keepers.

10. 45.

11. Yes, Bert Trautmann, goalkeeper for Manchester City.

12. Bobby Moore.

More Kings and Queens

1. Who was known as: (*a*) 'the Confessor'; (*b*) 'the Sun King'; (*c*) 'the Lionheart'?

2. Name the queen who ruled the Russian empire from 1762 to 1796.

3. Name three English kings killed by arrows. Can you say where they were killed?

4. (*a*) Who was the mother of Queen Elizabeth I? (*b*) Who was the only woman to be Queen of France and Scotland?

5. Which king worked for a time in the Royal Naval dockyard at Deptford and later forbade his subjects to grow beards?

6. Which kings or queens of England were never crowned?

7. What connection have Marshal Jean Baptiste Bernadotte of France and King Charles XIV of Sweden?

8. Who were: (*a*) Jenghiz Khan; (*b*) Kublai Khan; (*c*) Tamerlane?

9. What have these in common: Perkin Warbeck, Lambert Simnel, Duke of Monmouth?

10. Who was the first king of England from each of these: (*a*) Norman; (*b*) Plantagenet; (*c*) Tudor; (*d*) Stuart; (*e*) House of Hanover; (*f*) House of Windsor?

11. Which English king was responsible for the dissolution of the monasteries?

12. Queen Victoria had four sons and five daughters. Can you give the names of at least one of each?

More Kings and Queens

1. (*a*) Edward, King of England, 1042–66; (*b*) Louis XIV of France; (*c*) Richard I of England.

2. Catherine the Great.

3. Harold at the battle of Hastings, 1066; William II in the New Forest, 1100; Richard I in France, 1199.

4. (*a*) Anne Boleyn; (*b*) Mary, Queen of Scots.

5. Peter the Great of Russia (1672–1725).

6. Since 1066 only three – Edward V, Lady Jane Grey and Edward VIII.

7. The same person.

8. (*a*) ruler of the Mongols (1162–1227) who conquered most of Asia; (*b*) grandson of Jenghiz Khan (1216–94), ruler of the Mongols and China; (*c*) son of a Mongol chieftain (1336–1405) who conquered Asia Minor.

9. They were all Pretenders to the English throne.

10. (*a*) William I; (*b*) Henry II;
    (*c*) Henry VII; (*d*) James I;
    (*e*) George I; (*f*) George V.

11. Henry VIII.

12. Edward VII; Alfred, Duke of Edinburgh; Arthur, Duke of Connaught; Leopold, Duke of Albany.
    Victoria; Alice; Helena; Louise; Beatrice.

More Quotations

1. Whose last words were: (a) 'All my possessions for a moment of time'; (b) 'My design is to make what haste I can to be gone'; (c) 'I must sleep now'; (d) 'Remember!'?

2. Who wrote: (a) 'A little learning is a dangerous thing'; (b) 'Knowledge comes, but wisdom lingers'?

3. Which Prime Minister said: (a) 'My lips are sealed'; (b) 'You have never had it so good'; (c) 'Wait and see'; (d) 'Give us the tools and we will finish the job'?

4. Who said of whom: 'He speaks to me as if I was a public meeting'?

5. Who said: (a) 'There is no sin except stupidity'; (b) 'Pleasure's a sin, and sometimes sin's a pleasure'; (c) 'A man does not sin by commission only but often by omission'?

6. What did Napoleon call 'a trade of barbarians'?

7. Whose last words were: (a) 'I shall hear in heaven'; (b) 'Don't let the awkward squad fire over my grave'; (c) 'So much to do – so little done!'; (d) 'I fear, gentlemen, I am an unconscionable time a-dying'?

8. Who said of whom: 'A sophistical rhetorician, inebriated with the exuberance of his own verbosity'?

9. What did Dr. Johnson say about: (a) a public library; (b) London?

10. Who said: 'Après-moi – le deluge'?

11. Keats wrote that 'a thing of beauty is . . .' – what?

12. Who said: 'When people agree with me I always feel that I must be wrong'?

More Quotations

1. (*a*) Queen Elizabeth I;   (*b*) Oliver Cromwell;
   (*c*) Lord Byron;   (*d*) King Charles I.

2. (*a*) Alexander Pope;   (*b*) Alfred Tennyson.

3. (*a*) Baldwin;   (*b*) Macmillan;
   (*c*) Asquith;   (*d*) Churchill.

4. Queen Victoria of Gladstone.

5. (*a*) Oscar Wilde;   (*b*) Lord Byron;
   (*c*) Marcus Aurelius.

6. War.

7. (*a*) Beethoven;   (*b*) Robert Burns;
   (*c*) Cecil Rhodes;   (*d*) King Charles II.

8. Disraeli of Gladstone.

9. (*a*) 'No place affords a more striking conviction of the vanity of human hopes'; (*b*) 'When a man is tired of London he is tired of life'.

10. King Louis XV.

11. 'a joy forever'.

12. Oscar Wilde.

More Sportsmen

1. Name the British tennis player who won the Wimbledon men's singles title three years in succession (1934–6).

2. With which sports do you associate: (a) 'Babe' Ruth; (b) Bobby Jones; (c) Sydney Wooderson; (d) Stirling Moss?

3. What was the result of William Webb Ellis picking up the ball and running with it while playing football in 1823?

4. (a) Which king of England rode his own horses at Newmarket? (b) Which king of England excelled at tennis? (c) Which future king played in the men's doubles at Wimbledon?

5. Which racing-driver won the World Drivers Championship the most times up to 1975?

6. What was the great achievement of Robert Tyre Jones?

7. What nationality were these tennis players: (a) Frank Sedgman; (b) Manuel Santana; (c) Jack Kramer; (d) Cliff Drysdale; (e) Lew Hoad; (f) Jan Kodes?

8. Why is Drysdale the odd one out of those above?

9. Which jockey won the Derby at his 27th attempt, six days after being knighted?

10. What golfing feat was achieved by Harry Vardon?

11. What rugby football distinction is held by Eric Ashton?

12. Where and when did Paavo Nurmi get twelve medals?

More Sportsmen

1. Fred Perry.

2. (*a*) baseball;   (*b*) golf;
   (*c*) athletics;   (*d*) motor-racing.

3. This incident brought about the development of rugby football.

4. (*a*) Charles II; (*b*) Henry VIII; (*c*) the Duke of York, the future George VI.

5. J. M. Fangio – five times between 1951 and 1957.

6. In 1930 he won the British and American Open Golf Championships and the British and American Amateur Championships.

7. (*a*) Australian;   (*b*) Spanish;
   (*c*) American;   (*d*) South African;
   (*e*) Australian;   (*f*) Czechoslovakian.

8. All the others have been men's singles champions at Wimbledon.

9. Sir Gordon Richards in 1953.

10. He won the British Open Championship six times.

11. He captained Wigan at Wembley in six Cup Finals in nine years (1958–66).

12. In the three Olympics of 1920, 1924 and 1928 – nine gold and three silver medals.

More Writers

1. Who was the first woman novelist and playwright?

2. What were the Christian names of: (*a*) Thackeray; (*b*) Chesterton; (*c*) Wells?

3. Which British Prime Minister was awarded the Nobel prize for literature?

4. Whose biography was written by: (*a*) James Boswell; (*b*) Mrs. Gaskell; (*c*) John Lockhart?

5. Which famous writer was declared bankrupt with debts of over £100,000?

6. Who was Petrarch, and who was Plutarch?

7. Who wrote these books: (*a*) *The Mill on the Floss*; (*b*) *Greenmantle*; (*c*) *Cranford*; (*d*) *Peter Simple*; (*e*) *The Way of all Flesh*; (*f*) *The Vicar of Wakefield*?

8. Name: (*a*) the British Prime Minister who wrote several novels; (*b*) the American general who wrote a famous religious novel; (*c*) the king of England who wrote a book attacking tobacco.

9. Who wrote: (*a*) *Catch-22*; (*b*) *Saturday Night and Sunday Morning*; (*c*) *The Cruel Sea*; (*d*) *The Flying Inn*?

10. Who created these characters: (*a*) James Bond; (*b*) Bertie Wooster; (*c*) William; (*d*) The Wombles?

11. What was the most famous work by: (*a*) Edward Gibbon; (*b*) T. E. Lawrence; (*c*) Jonathan Swift; (*d*) Izaak Walton?

12. Name the two famous works by Homer.

More Writers

1. Mrs. Aphra Behn (1640–89).

2. (*a*) William Makepeace;   (*b*) Gilbert Keith;
   (*c*) Herbert George.

3. Winston Churchill, in 1953.

4. (*a*) Samuel Johnson; (*b*) Charlotte Brontë; (*c*) Sir
   Walter Scott (also Burns and Napoleon).

5. Walter Scott.

6. Petrarch was a fourteenth-century lyric poet of Italy,
   and Plutarch (*c*. A.D. 46–120) was a Greek biographer
   famous for his *Parallel Lives*.

7. (*a*) George Eliot;   (*b*) John Buchan;
   (*c*) Mrs. Gaskell;   (*d*) Captain Marryat;
   (*e*) Samuel Butler;   (*f*) Oliver Goldsmith.

8. (*a*) Benjamin Disraeli;   (*b*) Lew Wallace;
   (*c*) James I.

9. (*a*) Joseph Heller;   (*b*) Alan Sillitoe;
   (*c*) Nicholas Monsarrat;   (*d*) G. K. Chesterton.

10. (*a*) Ian Fleming;   (*b*) P. G. Wodehouse;
    (*c*) Richmal Crompton;   (*d*) Elisabeth Beresford.

11. (*a*) *The History of the Decline and Fall of the Roman
    Empire*; (*b*) *The Seven Pillars of Wisdom*; (*c*) *Gulliver's
    Travels*; (*d*) *The Compleat Angler*.

12. The *Iliad* and the *Odyssey*.